SHOCK
JOCKS

Copyright © 2008 by Rory O'Connor

978-0-9752724-3-5

All rights reserved. No part of this book may be reproduced in any form, except brief excerpts for the purpose of review, without written permission of the publisher.

AlterNet Books
77 Federal Street, 2nd Floor
San Francisco, CA 94107
www.AlterNet.org
books@alternet.org

Cover by Robin Terra | terra studio
Cover Photographs:
    Rush Limbaugh & Bill O'Reilly: Getty Images; Michael Savage: Corbis;
    Sean Hannity & Don Imus: AP Images; Laura Ingraham: Rob Bluey

Interior by Daniel Ridge

Printed in the United States of America with 50% post-consumer recycled material and soy-based ink.

LIBRARY OF CONGRESS CATALOGING-IN-PUBLICATION DATA

O'Connor, Rory, 1951-
 Shock jocks : hate speech and talk radio : America's ten worst hate talkers and the progressive alternatives / Rory O'Connor with Aaron Cutler.
    p. cm.
 ISBN 978-0-9752724-3-5
1. Radio talk shows--United States. 2. Radio broadcasting--Political aspects--United States. 3. Radio in politics--United States. I. Cutler, Aaron, 1985- II. Title.

 PN1991.8.T35O26 2008
 384.54'43--dc22
                            2008010639

First printing, 2008

1 2 3 4 5 6 7 8 9 10 – 12 11 10 09 08

SHOCK JOCKS

HATE SPEECH & TALK RADIO

America's Ten Worst Hate Talkers
and the Progressive Alternatives

RORY O'CONNOR
with Aaron Cutler

This book
is dedicated to my two sons,
Ciaran and Aidan.

CONTENTS

CHAPTER THREE
The Top Ten Worst Shock Jocks (Minus Imus) 49

CHAPTER FOUR
Fear of Fairness 125

CHAPTER FIVE
Air Wars and Conservative Dominance 155

INTRODUCTION

America, We Have a Problem

Talk radio is running America. We have to deal with that problem.
—Senator Trent Lott

Comedian and television talk show host Jon Stewart once said of the CNN program *Crossfire*, "It's not so much that it's bad, as it's hurting America." The same can be said of the highly politicized, overly partisan and often factually challenged world of news-and-opinion talk radio. Many top talk show hosts, from the recently resurrected Don Imus to industry giants such as Rush Limbaugh and Sean Hannity, regularly employ and promote hate speech aimed against women, minorities, homosexuals, and foreigners over public airwaves, while simultaneously blurring the lines between entertainment, opinion, and journalism. Proclaiming that their antigay, antiwoman, and racially or ethnically charged remarks are merely meant as good-humored, inoffensive, and "politically incorrect" fun, these highly paid, hugely powerful, mostly male, and all-white "shock jocks" deliver one-sided, highly politicized versions of the news, influence our national conversation, and affect legislation on important social issues ranging from immigration to abortion. At the same time, they foster a climate of social acceptance of racist, sexist, homophobic, and xenophobic language and hate speech—one that inevitably leads to tolerance of acts of hatred.

Shock jocks' use of hate speech under the guise of free speech is only part of the talk radio problem facing America. Our democratic dialogue is also being hindered by a huge ideological imbalance in the medium. Conservative viewpoints have long dominated talk radio, one of the most popular, influential, and intrinsically democratic media formats in America. Why? There are nearly as many answers to that question as there are respondents, but it's long been clear that, politically speaking, the news-and-opinion talk radio universe tips overwhelmingly to the right.

One recent study by the Center for American Progress and the media reform group Free Press—both avowedly liberal organizations—shows that more than 90 percent of the talk on the radio dial during weekdays is given over to conservative programming. According to the CAP/FP report, 257 news and talk stations owned by America's top five commercial station owners broadcast more than 2,570 hours of conservative talk each weekday. Only 254 hours are dedicated to progressive talk—resulting in a 10-to-1 dominance of conservatives over progressives.

As we shall see, this conservative control of the commercial radio news-talk genre is the result of a combination of factors—some historical, some political, some commercial, and some structural. But this right-wing air dominance arose in large part from years of relentless deregulation and concomitant consolidation, which vastly altered the industry's structure and allowed companies to acquire more stations, and thus increased advertising revenue, in any given market. This abiding penchant for deregulation led to the emergence of a handful of large corporations that essentially control national radio programming distribution, including most of talk radio. The days of local owners who programmed for local audiences are gone; instead centralized behemoths like industry leader Clear Channel now own hundreds of individual stations and distribute similar syndicated fare to each. Although these companies license the use of the public airwaves, few make their programming decisions in the public interest. Left unchallenged, and generally sharing a worldview with those on the right (along with positions on important issues such as the environment, taxes, trade, etc.), executives focus instead on the corporations' own economic and political interests.

Another part of the talk radio problem is the clever and continual blurring of distinctions between news, opinion, and entertainment practiced by many leading talkers on the right. Sounding like journalists—while denying that they do—allows them to dodge responsibility for their provocative comments. It also inexorably leads to the dissolution of borders between fact, fiction, and fun, to the ultimate detriment of our democracy. We already live in an age of media scams and scandals, of fake news and sponsored opinion. Pretending that everything talk radio hosts like Rush Limbaugh say is just meaningless entertainment is but a convenient way to introduce false narratives, set up straw dogs like "illegal aliens" and "phony soldiers," and in general demonize anyone the right sees as "the other." How meaningless was it when Limbaugh led his self-described "dittoheads" to revolt against a sitting president and leaders of their own party, killing bipartisan immigration reform by glibly rebranding it "shamnesty"?

If such effective acts are merely entertainment, it will undoubtedly come as a surprise to their devoted audiences—yet most talk radio hosts are forthright in denying that they practice journalism. Interviews conducted for this book with talkers of differing backgrounds, pedigrees, and political persuasions yielded surprising unanimity. Cenk Uygur, host of the morning drive show *The Young Turks* on the progressive talk network Air America, bluntly stated, "I don't think that any of us, Rush or Michael Savage or Randi Rhodes or me, are journalists, are bringing you the news."

Uygur's colleagues on both sides of the political divide echo his thoughts. "Entertainment, period. It's not about right wing or left wing," said Stephanie Miller, host of a progressive program out of Los Angeles syndicated by Jones Radio Networks. "The minute that we think we're a political movement, we're dead." Conservative talker Mike Gallagher, whose syndicated program attracts nearly 4 million listeners weekly, agreed. "We're entertainers—not news, not journalists—broadcasters and entertainers with strong opinions. But our job is to entertain, to be funny, and to be compelling."

Entertaining people with strong opinions about the news (without actually reporting or gathering any) sounds easy...and on the face of it, hosting a talk radio program appears to *be* easy—so easy it seems anyone can do it. No particular professional training, educational achievements, prior experience, or even character references are required (witness the recent return to radio of former Providence, Rhode Island, mayor Vincent "Buddy" Cianci Jr. following his release from federal custody after more than four years in prison for corruption). But while it may be true that anyone *can* do it, very few people can do it *well*.

In fact, being behind the microphone can sometimes be the "loneliest spot in the world," as *Los Angeles Times* reporter William Lobdell discovered during a stint as a fill-in host for conservative talker Hugh Hewitt, whose show is picked up by more than 100 stations throughout the country. "You wouldn't think being a talk radio show host would be all that tough; just read a few newspaper, magazine, and Web articles others have slaved to produce and then riff about them," Lobdell wrote. "But here's the hard part. It's just you, your voice, and the microphone. You are giving a monologue in an empty studio. You can't see your audience or sense their engagement. It felt like being locked in a sensory-deprivation chamber. Time seemed to slow, the awful way it does during a car accident."

Even worse, the technical aspects of hosting also "flummoxed" the reporter. "My producer kept barking instructions in my ear, messing up what little rhythm I had going. I had to put callers on the air, a seemingly simple task that resulted in several hang-ups and accompanying dial tones that made the air waves," Lobdell recalled. "And I had to be constantly aware of the time, making sure the show broke away smoothly for commercial breaks and news (another failure). Though I was clearly a dead host talking, the callers and e-mailers, smelling blood, went after me with a disturbing glee."

David Foster Wallace made a similar assessment in "Host," a 2005 *Harper's Magazine* profile of John Ziegler, another popular right-leaning radio talker. "Hosting talk radio is an exotic, high-pressure gig that not many people are fit for, and being truly good at it requires skills so specialized that many of them don't have names," Wallace noted. "The fact of the matter is that it is not John Ziegler's job to be responsible, or nuanced, or to think about whether his on-air comments are productive or dangerous, or cogent, or even defensible...he has exactly one on-air job, and that is to be stimulating."

Wallace's point, which is usually "overlooked by people who complain about propaganda, misinformation, and irresponsibility in commercial talk radio," was precisely that Ziegler "is not a journalist—he is an entertainer." The same is said of Limbaugh, the most popular and influential radio talker of all time, and of literally hundreds of his industry peers and descendants. Wallace added that Limbaugh, Ziegler, and their ilk are more properly viewed as "part of a peculiar, modern, and very popular type of news industry, one that manages to enjoy the authority and influence of journalism without the stodgy constraints of fairness, objectivity, and responsibility that make trying to tell the truth such a drag for everyone involved."

Despite the medium's many current controversies and partisan political battles, and whether you choose to view it as entertainment or journalism, news or opinion, or all of the above, one fact is clear: Americans love to listen to talk radio. We also apparently love to talk back; every week, tens of millions of us engage in a robust, ongoing national conversation with our favored hosts on one of the most controversial niches in the ever-expanding modern media universe. By any measure—political, social, cultural, economic—talk radio is hot.

In commercial terms, although radio is one of the oldest forms of modern media, it is paradoxically still profitable. Despite competition from emerging technologies in recent years, the radio industry had a particularly prosperous year in 2005, posting its largest gain in advertising revenue since 1988, and in 2006, the 20 percent industrywide profit margin was the third-highest in the last 40 years. Every year, this dean of electronic media continues to produce billions in annual revenue—more than $20 billion overall, up from $12 billion in 1996, the year the Clinton administration and Congress combined to produce the first major overhaul of telecommunications law in more than 60 years.

Talk radio is even hotter in sociopolitical and cultural terms; it sometimes seems as if whatever our leading talk show hosts are saying or doing ranks among the most important national topics of the day. In many cases the radio talkers are actually discussing important national topics, such as race and ethnicity, and war and peace, but there seems equally to be a weird and growing national obsession over the politics, personalities, and piques of the many men and the few women who regularly harangue, cajole, insult, incite, inflame, delight, entertain, inform, and misinform us over the public airwaves.

Consider just a few of the numerous talk radio–related news events during the last half of 2007, for example. Rush Limbaugh consistently made fresh headlines while causing new controversies, even as he celebrated his program's 19th anniversary. Whether he was smearing a 12-year-old health care recipient, attacking antiwar service members as "phony soldiers" and "suicide bombers," being castigated on the floor of Congress for doing so, and then raising millions of dollars for children of "fallen Marines" by auctioning a letter denouncing him for his remarks, or simply contemplating the impending end of his probation for a narcotics arrest ("My five weeks in rehab at The Meadows were among the best times in my life," Limbaugh told the *Palm Beach Post*. "I would recommend it even to people who are not addicted"), the 24-hour news cycle seemed to be stuck on "All Rush, all the time." The first part of 2008 proved no different; Limbaugh's objections to Republican presidential candidate John McCain and his supposedly "liberal" stance on issues such as immigration and campaign finance reform resulted in massive attention from mainstream media outlets, which effectively promoted both his personality and his program.

Meanwhile, fellow top-rated, nationally syndicated talkers such as Bill O'Reilly and Michael Savage competed for public attention by endlessly indulging in outrage. O'Reilly first compared the progressive political Web site Daily Kos to the Nazi Party and the Ku Klux Klan, then expressed his amazement that a world-famous Harlem restaurant "was exactly the same" as other restaurants in New York, "even though it's run by blacks." ("There wasn't one person...who was screaming, 'MF-er, I want more iced tea,'" the racist radio ranter added.) Savage, who despite his base in liberal San Francisco veers further to the right than either O'Reilly or Limbaugh, was condemned unanimously by that city's board of supervisors for his use of "defamatory language" against immigrants. The resolution came in response to a broadcast in which Savage remarked of a group of students fasting in support of changes in immigration policy, "Let them fast until they starve to death. Then that solves the problem."

Such caustic comments by leading talk radio hosts, shocking as they may seem, were nothing new to their avid audiences, and the brouhaha they created was as usual quite positive for them and their ratings. In fact, talk radio hosts must be either extraordinarily unlucky or extremely untimely in their remarks to suffer any lasting negative consequences. Rarely, and then owing only to an unusual confluence of events, certain on-air statements are suddenly and mysteriously deemed "over the line" or "going too far." Representatives of the corporations that license the airwaves to broadcast those remarks then roundly deplore them. Less frequently, and only when executives face prolonged public pressure and open advertiser revolt, do they first suspend and then occasionally (but hardly ever) actually dismiss the offender. Even then, the punishment never seems to last long.

Thus what happened to shock jock Don Imus after his notorious "nappy headed ho's" insult to the Rutgers University women's basketball team is just the exception that proves the rule...and even Imus wasn't banished from the airwaves for very long. The entire Imus affair (closely followed by the suspension of fellow shock jocks Opie and Anthony for making on-air sexually offensive "jokes" about Secretary of State Condoleezza Rice, First Lady Laura Bush, and for good measure, the Queen of England) merely highlighted the fact that such controversial remarks and on-air forays into out-and-out racism, sexism, sacrilege, homophobia, and generalized bigotry are really the mother's milk of talk radio. Far from being singular, Don Imus is actually the poster boy for all that is wrong with our most popular populist media.

Imus supporters regularly insist that none of what he or other shock jocks say really matters, since it supposedly "isn't serious." Can't we all just *lighten up* and *move on*? Stop being so *politically correct* and *humorless*? If you don't like what's on the air, why not *change the station* or simply *stop listening*? But it's not enough just to change the station. That station's message is being broadcast daily by networks that reach tens of millions of listeners over airwaves that are literally publicly owned—that belong, in other words, to all of us, including all the human beings who are regularly the butt of insults, including *brillohead, dark meat, Mandingo, Uncle Ben, gook, chink, slanty-eyed bastard, queer, homo, ho, lesbo, gorilla*, and *pimp*.

There should of course be a place in our society, and on our airwaves, for those who play the part of court jester and alter ego, whose stock-in-trade is saying aloud those things others dare speak only in private or *sotto voce*. But there should also be a special burden placed on those using the public airwaves, one that calls for care and concern about the context in which they're speaking. All of us, even the so-called "shock jocks," have a responsibility to act for the greater good, and talk radio shouldn't be used as a vehicle to stir up old hatreds and divide us as a nation.

Many radio listeners want to believe that none of this loose talk actually hurts anyone—but most African Americans and women didn't say "lighten up" or "move on" or "don't be so politically correct" when Don Imus described the Rutgers University women's basketball team in crude and cruel, racist and sexist terms. In a society where hate crimes are on the rise, and where nooses are still displayed as racial threats, hate speech doesn't customarily elicit that reaction from the people most directly affected by it. But no one can afford to stand back and be neutral; it is incumbent on us all to take a stand and confront hate speech wherever and whenever it is heard. "People want to believe that it's 'just words' and that we as a society are past racism, past sexism, and the epidemic of violence against women," talk radio host Laura Flanders explained in the course of research for this book. "But we're not, so there is no *neutral* context for comments like that. It's real-life people putting real-life obstacles in front of each other. Let's not be afraid of that debate, to make those criticisms."

AMERICA, WE HAVE A PROBLEM

So who *are* America's leading talk show hosts, and what are they saying? What impact is the medium having on politics and culture, and on such real-world issues as immigration, taxation, and the ongoing occupation of Iraq? Is it fair to assume that "political" talk radio is largely motivated by ideology? Or is talk radio more properly understood as just a business, driven by revenue and profits? Do conservatives dominate today's airwaves because they generate high ratings and thus high advertising rates and profits, or because the corporations that distribute their programming benefit politically from doing so? How do the corporations that distribute and sponsor their programs decide who gets on and stays on the public airwaves? What are the progressive alternatives? Should we try to ensure that core journalistic values such as fairness, balance, and factual accuracy are reflected in what many say, after all is done and said, is an entertainment-driven medium? Or does such concern and intervention instead do harm to the principle of free speech, one of our most cherished and valuable rights?

More than any other mass medium, radio has a captive audience, in part because the majority of its members are listening in their cars during commute times. But in any given large market, those "captives" now enjoy the freedom of literally dozens of choices of what to listen to, ranging from AM stations to FM to podcasts to satellite radio. As a result, even the most successful talk radio station captures just 5 to 6 percent of the total listening audience. In these days of "narrow-casting," such a niche can still prove lucrative for both the talk show hosts and the corporations that distribute their programs. As a result, there's high demand for those few individuals who can actually deliver a sizable audience. With that audience comes influence and power, not only to comment on but also actually to effect events of importance to us all as citizens in a democracy.

An increasing number of Americans now agree with Senator Trent Lott and numerous other close industry observers and media watchdogs that the power and influence of America's leading radio talk show hosts is at best problematic and at its worst dangerous to democracy. Now that even Republican leaders (including President George W. Bush) have begun feeling the heat from right-wing talk radio, it's time for an objective, comprehensive look at the history, issues, and personalities behind this media and political phenomenon that attracts tens of millions of listeners and generates billions of dollars for its practitioners and their corporate overlords.

In turn both frightening and fascinating, talk radio occupies a peculiar place on the broadening spectrum of media choices. Although most mass media are increasingly controlled by a handful of corporations, never before have so many different news sources been so widely and readily accessible. Greater consolidation has paradoxically been paralleled by increased fragmentation and a seeming surfeit of news and information choices. Yet this increasing fragmentation has also resulted in an increasing number of ideological rather than objective or professional news outlets, "a kind of epistemic free-for-all in which 'the truth' is wholly a matter of perspective and agenda," as David Foster Wallace elegantly phrased it. Although greater choice theoretically seems to be a societal good, in reality it has led us instead to an ever-greater reliance on partisan news sources that serve only to bear out what we already believe to be true. As a result, as Wallace noted, "it is increasingly hard to determine which sources to pay attention to and how exactly to distinguish real information from spin."

And therein lies the true problem of talk radio. Rush Limbaugh's original but toxic mix of news, entertainment, and unbalanced analysis has become the national model, setting a much-imitated standard and initiating a race to the bottom. "The mainstream media is biased against us," the right-wing talkers maintain; thus the need for unbiased (aka politically conservative) talk radio to restore the missing balance—mostly by dismissing as biased any other media that departs from the common talking points heard daily on talk radio. This solipsistic thesis simultaneously extends conservatives' distrust of the so-called liberal media and exalts talk radio as the necessary antidote.

So yes, America, we've got a problem. Talk radio is too valuable—and too political—to be left solely in the hands of shock jocks. How can we as a free society—one that loves to talk and to listen, and then to talk back—ensure that talk radio is finally opened up to as many voices as possible? How can we enshrine free speech as both an ideal and a reality on our publicly owned airwaves?

CHAPTER 1

The Resurrection of Don Imus

The more money you make your employer,
the more free speech you get. —John Ziegler

In early November 2007, executives of the Citadel Broadcasting Corporation announced that they had hired the disgraced radio talk show host, Don Imus. The comeback meant Imus would soon return to the airwaves during the "morning drive" time slot— moving from the CBS-owned WFAN-AM to WABC-AM in New York—in the same time slot and in the same city where his nationally syndicated *Imus in the Morning* program had been based, and then banished, some six months earlier. The resurrection of the self-styled "I-Man" was complete.

His many previous transgressions were apparently forgiven— the most recent and notable being his infamous on-air characterization of the young, predominantly African American women of the Rutgers University women's basketball team as "nappy-headed ho's." The Rutgers remark, combined with a sudden perfect media storm facilitated by the Internet and cable television's relentlessly single-focus 24/7 news cycle, ultimately led Imus's corporate bosses at CBS and NBC (owners of the cable channel MSNBC, which simulcast his radio program) first to suspend and later to fire him. Ironically, the shock jock was dismissed for doing precisely what he was hired to do: insult, entertain, shock, and outrage, thus creating controversy, boosting ratings, and making money for himself and everyone connected to him and his program.

Months after the fact, Imus's racist and sexist observation about the Rutgers basketball team still seemed freshly offensive to many. Officials with the National Association of Black Journalists, for example, an organization representing more than 3,000 journalists nationwide, said they remained outraged and questioned why any broadcast company would enable Imus "to continue his history of racial insults." NABJ president Barbara Ciara added, "To put him back on the air now makes light of his serious and offensive racial remarks that are still ringing in the ears of people all over this country." Nevertheless, the man even the normally staid Associated Press had taken to calling the "Rasputin of radio" was back from the brink and, as the AP noted, "poised to do it again."

Imus and his production team had been beating down the defenseless for cheap laughs for years before the Rutgers comment created a firestorm of controversy. Moreover, their litany of loutish remarks and accompanying locker room behavior had been well documented for years, most notably by reporter Philip Nobile, who along with others at the nonprofit liberal news site TomPaine.com, had chronicled the serial abuse of minorities, women, homosexuals, and foreigners that had long passed for humor on the *Imus in the Morning* program.

From time to time, the I-Man himself addressed the issue of whether such remarks were wrong, both on his own program and elsewhere. He dismissed any and all objections, employing a cunning combination of excuses and rationales for the remarks. Sometimes he blamed "political correctness" for the controversy; alternately he declared the remarks were made by "an idiot," called them an aberration, cited his charity work with "black kids with cancer" as a defense against charges of racism; and then concluded, as many of his loyal listeners did, that if one found the comments objectionable, the appropriate response was simply to "not listen," to "change the dial" and to "move on."

One such exchange took place February 25, 2001, on *Imus in the Morning*:

Don Imus: Bo Dietl (a frequent Imus guest) called me yesterday, and he wanted to apologize for some things he said yesterday on the program. I think he was surprised that I wasn't angry with him, and I'm not angry with him. But I don't know what to do. I mean you either don't put him on, or if you do put him on, you take what you get. His use of the word "gook" I guess offended a number of people. It's just not good. Why we tolerate that is just, I guess if I thought that he were bigoted or racist, then I wouldn't tolerate it. He's not. But he's an idiot. He's not an idiot, he doesn't care. He doesn't think of that word perhaps as you or I do. He just thinks it's amusing. To some people it's not amusing. Some people, hurts their feelings. Other than Rick Kaplan or one of these fat pig decorators who works for us, I really don't want to hurt anybody's feelings. I actually don't. So anyway, he said he's sorry. He's not. He's sorry

I guess if you were offended. I just think you have to move on. I think the thing probably to do is not listen if you're offended.

Imus producer **Bernard McGuirk** (imitating Dietl): Let me say to all you gooks out there, sorry.

Another occurred a year earlier on CNN's *Larry King Live*. Jeff Greenfield, a news analyst and one of the many media luminaries who frequently appeared as a guest on *Imus in the Morning*, was filling in for King as host and interviewing Imus. Greenfield wondered aloud about the many prominent personalities who continually appeared on the Imus program, while ignoring its host's penchant for racist, sexist, homophobic, and xenophobic commentary.

Jeff Greenfield: It is interesting to me, though, that when Bob Grant, a radio personality in New York, referred to the former mayor, an African American, as a washroom attendant, he was fired by ABC. And yet, on your show, people like Anna Quindlen, Senator Bill Bradley, the vice president of the United States, Joe Lieberman, people—prominent journalists and not-so-prominent journalists come on your show....

Imus: You can cite two or three examples over 30 years. Thirty years I've been on the radio—of stuff that's been offensive. Because, you know, I got black kids with cancer coming out to this ranch in New Mexico who don't think I'm a racist. And the people who are accusing me of being a racist haven't [given a dime] to any charity in their lifetime....I mean, it offends me, and I'm not going to put up with it. I don't put up with it. It's silly.

Greenfield failed to challenge Imus's claim of only "two or three examples over 30 years...of stuff that's been offensive," but he easily could have. A minute of basic research by CNN staffers would have revealed that the statement was laughably false. Although Imus may not have called the former mayor of New York a washroom attendant (for which fellow shock jock Bob Grant was deservedly fired), he did call *New York Times* White House correspondent Gwen Ifill (also an African American) a "cleaning lady," as *New York Daily News* columnist Lars-Erik Nelson reported in 1998.

While Greenfield mused on-air about why prominent politicians and journalists continually appeared on the Imus show and didn't "seem to have a problem" with his offensive remarks, a glance at an article by Ken Auletta published two years earlier in the *New Yorker* would have instantly enlightened him. Imus is "the second most powerful person in the country in terms of selling books," Auletta wrote, quoting a top Simon and Schuster executive. The publisher credited the shock jock with boosting his company's print order for *Washington Post*/CNN media critic Howard Kurtz's book *Spin Cycle* from 25,000 copies to 200,000. (Denying any conflict of interest, Kurtz once explained in a *Washington Post* chat room exchange, "I don't believe [as a regular listener and very occasional guest on the program] that Imus is in any way racist. He sometimes crosses the line, as he himself would admit, in trying to make people laugh, but it's all shtick. He's no bigot.") The real motivation for Kurtz's willful blindness was perhaps better explained by the novelist and onetime *New York Times* columnist Anna Quindlen, who, when speaking of the market power of Imus, told Auletta, "All you need do is hear him wax poetic about your book and you say, 'Hell, I'd buy that book.'"

Auletta concluded, "Five mornings a week, from 5:30 to 10, *Imus in the Morning* takes care of his 'guys'—promoting their books, their columns, and their lives to more than ten million listeners on more than a hundred stations and on MSNBC-TV." The payback? "The program generates nearly half of the $50 million a year in revenue, which WFAN contributes to its corporate parent, CBS Radio."

Auletta charitably went on to note, "It's unfair, no doubt, to suggest that those who go on the air with Imus, or donate to the ranch, are doing so solely out of self-interest...journalists who spend airtime with Imus have many motives for doing so." He quoted Greenfield in the article as saying, "For a lot of people, going on Imus is a way for them to be a different person." Greenfield told Auletta he often got more comments for his Imus appearances than for his own television work.

"I think people are onto the political-journalistic dance. They know when they watch a press conference or an interview show they are getting predigested stuff—people are saying the same things they always say. With Imus, people feel he's going to ask them blunt things and not take bullshit for an answer," Greenfield reasoned. "In that way, people who talk to Imus are selling themselves as personalities, far removed from, say, the confines of a scripted newscast," Auletta explained. "The television anchors Tom Brokaw and Dan Rather are regulars; another is Mike Wallace, of *60 Minutes,* who says, 'You get to feel like you're a member of his club.'"

Wallace's remark calls to mind Groucho Marx's famous quote, "I don't care to belong to any club that will have me as a member." Wallace in particular should have known better; he had exposed on *60 Minutes* Imus's use of the word "nigger" just a year before speaking with Auletta.

Prominent *Imus in the Morning* "club members" such as Wallace, Greenfield, Brokaw, and Rather really had no excuse for ignoring the continual depredations of the Imus crew (Philip Nobile cited a "gentleman's agreement among elite journalists in the Boston–Washington corridor regarding morning radio man Don Imus"), since they had been widely reported, not only repeatedly and exhaustively on TomPaine.com but also in leading outlets such as *60 Minutes* and the *New Yorker*.

John Moyers, son of famed journalist Bill Moyers, founded TomPaine.com in 1999 and ran the site until 2003. One of TomPaine.com's most popular series was a group of articles written by Nobile condemning talk radio host Don Imus for sexist, racist, and bigoted remarks in 2000—years before his comments about the Rutgers University women's basketball team. One of Nobile's major points was that Imus got away with saying outrageous things because few in the mainstream media were willing to condemn him.

Nobile noted, "Just about anything goes—from saying that [African American basketball player] Larry Johnson ruined [white female TV news personality] Willow Bay for white men, to asking the borough president of the Bronx if he felt 'like the mayor of Mogadishu.'" As Nobile detailed, references to "gooks, chinks, slanty-eyed bastards, queers, homos, ho's, lesbos, gorillas, pimps, knuckle-dragging" African Americans, and the like abounded on Imus's program.

Asked why Imus was given such a free ride, John Moyers explained in an interview for this book that "media and political figures leveraged his notoriety, which he gained through his racist/sexist/homophobic shtick, to sell books, ideas, and so on. Essentially, they wanted to reach his audience with their wares. So they looked the other way and didn't pay much attention to what he said before they went on-air; in other words, they made it their business *not* to know. Howie Kurtz said nobody cared, and we were taking it too personally—he just followed the crowd. My own sense is that these people simply thought, 'Anything for that audience.'"

As TomPaine.com executive editor Isaiah J. Poole later wrote, "A lot of people who consider themselves reputable—both Democratic and Republican politicians, political consultants, journalists, and pundits—have shacked up in this seedy AM radio motel as if it were a five-star forum for serious political discourse. They knew better, as did the advertisers who bankrolled this enterprise and the networks that broadcast it. They have no one to blame but themselves for the soil on their own images as a result and for whatever consequences they face if they go back in."

Despite Imus's abysmal track record, for years executives at CBS and NBC saw nothing wrong with distributing his program. Nor did the many media and political personalities who accepted the I-Man's excuses for on-air bigotry—in exchange for reaching his audience of millions—express any objections. "Politicians who want our votes and journalists who want our trust should not be appearing on these shows; if they do, ask why they consented to be on a program that has regularly broadcast slurs against people of color, women, and gays and lesbians," Poole wrote in 2007, in the wake of the "nappy-headed ho's" incident, calling on radio listeners to "make advertisers feel uncomfortable for being associated with such shows, especially those that have refused to support progressive radio alternatives."

It was only when advertisers finally began deserting *Imus in the Morning* after the Rutgers remark—coupled with nonstop media attention and open employee revolt against executives at the corporations that had distributed, promoted, and protected Imus for so long—that the man who had previously appeared immune to shame or pressure was suddenly toppled. The most surprising result of the entire affair, in fact, was that after first merely "deploring" their shock jock's latest shocking remark, CBS and NBC executives were finally dragged, kicking and screaming, by audience, advertiser, and employee protest initially to suspend, and ultimately to fire, the I-Man and Company.

Now the I-Man is ba-a-a-a-ack—having been pilloried, paid penance, and paid off in the time-honored tradition of American scandal. Predictably, his new bosses said they were "ecstatic" to have him. "Don's unique brand of humor, knowledge of the issues, and ability to attract big-name guests is unparalleled," said WABC president and general manager Steve Borneman. "He is rested, fired up, and ready to do great radio."

Citadel Broadcasting CEO Farid Suleman added, "He didn't break the law. He's more than paid the price for what he did." (Suleman and Imus go way back—Suleman was previously the chief executive of Infinity Radio, which owned WFAN, the flagship for the nationally syndicated and simulcast *Imus in the Morning*, before Infinity merged with CBS Radio.)

The Las Vegas–based Citadel, which acquired numerous ABC radio stations from Walt Disney Company in 2006, now owns more than 240 radio stations around the country. Its 50,000-watt flagship station WABC already airs such top-ranked, nationally syndicated right-wing talkers as Rush Limbaugh, Sean Hannity, and Mark Levin—a "galaxy of stars," according to station manager Borneman, who also said Imus was "certainly an amazing addition to our station and for our company." Phil Boyce, vice president of news-talk programming for Citadel, gushed to the *New York Times*, "The chance to get Don is something we couldn't pass up." Boyce also said he expected other Citadel radio affiliates to carry Imus but declined to identify which ones.

Michael Harrison of the trade publication *Talkers Magazine* explained one reason why Citadel executives were so ecstatic about bringing Imus back to the airwaves. "He's more valuable now than before the controversy...He's in a position to sort of reinvent himself—to make himself more pertinent and even more interesting," Harrison told the Associated Press. "We are in a society where celebrity is the most important part of fame. Whether it's for good or for bad—that doesn't seem to translate in corporate America's unending quest for ratings."

Another reason for the executive ecstasy: putting Imus in the morning drive slot at WABC could increase Citadel's revenue by as much as $20 million, according to reliable industry estimates. *Ad Age* estimated in April 2007 that revenues for *Imus in the Morning* had brought in $15 million to $22 million for CBS's WFAN alone, with an additional $2.5 million on the MSNBC cable simulcast. When it comes to talk radio—as with virtually all other American media—money talks, usually louder than anything else.

WABC station representatives confirmed they would bring back much of the previous Imus cast, including longtime news anchor Charles McCord. No mention was made of fellow cast member Bernard McGuirk, whose hateful observations often spurred Imus to respond and whose own remarks about the Rutgers women's basketball team provoked the comment that got Team Imus fired in the first place. It seemed safe to assume, however, that McGuirk would return. After all, the show wouldn't be the same without him...

Imus's supporters often argue that he is "more liberal" than the other conservatives who dominate talk radio, since his guests include slightly left-of-center media luminaries such as Greenfield (now of CBS News), Frank Rich of the *New York Times* and David Gregory, Andrea Mitchell, and Tim Russert of NBC News, along with political bigwigs and former Democratic presidential hopefuls like Senators Joe Lieberman, John Kerry, and Bob Kerrey. Still, the political dimensions of the latest round of hirings and firings at WABC seem clear. The new Imus show will replace *Curtis and Kuby*, a more balanced program that in fact rated more highly than the previous Imus show on WFAN, which aired opposite it. Featuring conservative Guardian Angels founder Curtis Sliwa and radical left lawyer Ron Kuby, *Curtis and Kuby* was WABC's drive-time show for nearly eight years.

"I've had a fantastic, great run," cohost Kuby told reporters, after he was summarily told one afternoon not to bother showing up the next morning. "Our show has enjoyed the best audience—intelligent, compassionate, decent, and kind," Kuby added pointedly. "The new owners don't want that kind of show." Citadel honcho Boyce said he hoped to find another place on the WABC schedule for the conservative Sliwa, but none for Kuby, a renowned civil rights lawyer and onetime protégé of the fiery William Kunstler. When asked to explain, Boyce would make no further comment.

But were "the new owners" really new? Or was it true instead that when Imus met the new bosses, they were almost literally the same as the old bosses? As noted, Citadel CEO Farid Suleman had previously been the chief executive of Infinity Radio, which owned the Imus flagship station WFAN before merging with CBS Radio.

Further, what appeared at first glance to be a sale to Citadel of ABC Radio assets by the parent Walt Disney Company was in reality a merger. As the Wikipedia entry on Citadel Broadcasting notes, "On February 6, 2006, Forstmann Little and the Walt Disney Company agreed to merge Citadel with Disney's ABC Radio. Shares representing 57 percent of Citadel were distributed to shareholders of the Walt Disney Company following the company's acquisition of 22 stations from ABC Radio." After the merger, Citadel's ownership structure was made up of Disney shareholders (57 percent); Forstmann Little (27 percent); and former Citadel shareholders, exclusive of Forstmann Little (16 percent).

The deal put cash into Disney's coffers in exchange for radio stations, but it may also have been designed in part to obscure continued control of the airwaves by the media giant's shareholders behind a holding company. As Citadel Broadcasting's Web site notes, the company is "the largest pure play radio company in the United States, with a strong national footprint reaching more than 50 markets. Our company is comprised of 177 FM stations and 66 AM stations in the nation's leading markets. In addition to our strong national footprint, Citadel Broadcasting owns and operates ABC Radio Networks, which creates and distributes programming to more than 4,000 affiliates." The multibillion-dollar cash and stock transaction that led to the acquisition of ABC Radio made Citadel the third-largest station owner in the United

States. (This status may not last long: financial analysts speculate the company will "slim down" both costs and people at ABC Radio, then spin off individual stations. As one observer noted, "Big leveraged finance guys" whose interests "are short-term, not long-term" are bankrolling Citadel.)

So maybe, in addition to Citadel Broadcasting CEO Suleman, the new Imus bosses *are* in fact the old bosses…but, however tangled the ownership of the I-Man's new radio home may seem, the response to his return to the airwaves was entirely predictable. Supporters and enablers hailed his resurrection. Prominent guests, such as former senator Kerrey, vowed to return to the Imus airwaves in support of their friend. Meanwhile, outraged critics, such as those from the NABJ and the National Organization for Women, told the press that the idea of Imus returning to the airwaves was "nearly as insulting as the crude comments that took him off the air." Al Sharpton, who played a predictably prominent and recurrent role in the entire affair, demanded that Citadel executives meet with advertisers and minority groups to explain how the company plans to prevent a return by Imus to "his former vile and biased behavior." Sharpton announced, "Mr. Imus has the right to make a living, but we have the right to make sure he does not come back to disrupt our living."

Although no financial details were forthcoming about the new Imus-Citadel deal, "making a living" is not a real concern for Imus under any circumstances. Just before his dismissal, he had signed a five-year, $40 million contract with CBS. (According to his attorney, Martin Garbus, the contract contained a clause in which CBS acknowledged that his services were "unique, extraordinary, irreverent, intellectual, topical, controversial," and that such programming was "desired by company" and "consistent with company rules and policy.") Imus threatened to sue for $120 million after he was fired and then settled in August 2007 for an undisclosed amount of money presumed to be in the millions. No details were offered at the time about either the future national syndication of the WABC broadcast or any companion television deal, although the previous *Imus in the Morning* program aired nationally on more than 60 stations, as well as on the MSNBC cable network.

The latest Imus "resurrection" is certainly not the first (and probably not the last) in his decades-long career. On May 17, 2000, a week after a TomPaine.com advertisement about Imus's remarks ran on the op-ed page of the *New York Times*, the I-Man made an on-air pledge to refrain from his sexist, racist, and homophobic shtick. After first raging against TomPaine.com and a follow-up piece in *Time* headlined "Imus 'n' Andy" and then insisting, "I'm not going to change this program because some punk runs an ad" (while adding that he was "as opposed to racism and bigotry and homophobia as anybody"), Imus folded in the face of objections from such prominent African Americans as newspaper columnist Clarence Page. Vowing to forswear his racist parodies, sexually charged epithets, and anti-ethnic comments, Imus promised Page, "I'll do the best I can with your pledge and rein in these renegades, OK?"

A year later, Philip Nobile again monitored *Imus in the Morning* for several months to see how the I-Man was faring. As Nobile wrote on the TomPaine.com Web site, "The result, in brief: Imus broke his pledge. His stone-cold bigotry is back, as creepy as ever. And his bodyguard of big-name media and political guests, strategically deaf to the show's lower frequencies, have hung in as well."

THE RESURRECTION OF DON IMUS

Given his record of serial transgressions, it seems safe to conclude that Imus's latest fall from grace will not be his last. In the meantime, who will profit from his current return from the dead? First and foremost come the restored I-Man and his wrecking crew. Ever close on their heels are the media corporations that broadcast his program and the single-focus executives who operate them, and the political and media elite who are willing to tolerate the I-Man's intolerance in exchange for access to his audience.

The Unpleasant Aftertaste of Craig Carton

When CBS Radio executives announced that they had finally found permanent replacements for the fired on-air team at *Imus in the Morning*, few questioned their decision to hire former professional athlete and current sports broadcaster Boomer Esiason as a host of a revamped sports and news talk show on WFAN. But in the wake of the Imus program's history of racism, sexism, and homophobia, no one expected them to name as Esiason's sidekick Craig Carton, someone almost as controversial and offensive as Imus himself.

Carton's rap sheet included, according to *Newsday*, "perceived insults of Asians, Hispanics, Poles, gays, Catholics, Italians, Jews, women...and various politicians." His inventory of insults is lengthy: he called on his listeners to turn suspected undocumented immigrants—including their friends and neighbors—over to immigration authorities. He said women suffering postpartum depression "must be crazy in the first place." Carton and his cohost Ray Rossi regularly outed politicians as gay or lesbian and allowed callers to air their own unsubstantiated claims. Referring to Jun Choi, a Korean American mayoral candidate who ran for mayor of Edison, New Jersey, in 2005, Carton said, in a stereotypical Asian accent, "I don't care if the Chinese population in Edison has quadrupled in the last year. Chinese should never dictate the outcome of an election. Americans should."

Among the politicians who denounced Carton and Rossi's antics was New Jersey state senator Ray Lesniak, who noted, "Those guys are dangerous. You can't ignore that kind of hate speech.

You have to stand up to it." Lesniak had firsthand experience with Carton's bigotry. After he protested Carton's statement in which he said, "Half the Polacks joined the Nazis to do what? Kill Jews," the host called him a "Jew-hating bastard."

An industry veteran, Carton has achieved ratings success virtually everywhere he's worked in the past. His program in New Jersey boasted an audience larger than that of any other afternoon talk show host on FM radio. Carton began his broadcasting career in 1991 at WGR Radio in Buffalo, New York, where his show quickly became a hit. He then moved from Buffalo to Cleveland in 1992 and to Philadelphia sports leader WIP-AM a year later. During more than four years at WIP, Carton's program soared in the ratings.

From there, Carton's career took off. In 1997, he was hired to host a syndicated sports talk show that aired on 40 stations throughout the country. He then joined KKFN in Denver as morning show host. In his first year with the station, his program became the highest-rated show in the station's history. When cross-town rival KBPI later hired him, *that* program then became the highest-rated local morning show in Denver. Following a short stint at WNEW-FM in New York City, Carton joined WKXW New Jersey 101.5, where he spent more than five years hosting *The Jersey Guys* during afternoon drive time.

Despite his rap sheet—or perhaps because of it, and the high ratings it engendered—Carton is well regarded within the radio talk show industry. He was selected as one of the top 100 most important and influential talk show hosts in the country for three straight years by *Talkers Magazine*. Radio and Records nominated him as 2006 talk show host of the year, and he won virtually every major radio award in the Garden State. His stated broadcasting philosophy: "Keep it real and get a reaction, whether you make them laugh, or you make them cry, or you make them happy, or you make them sad. Be relevant." (The *Jersey Guys* Web site said, perhaps more accurately, that the show's purpose was to spread insults over the airwaves.)

Why would CBS turn to such a controversial personality in the wake of the Imus imbroglio? In a statement announcing that Carton would join Boomer Esiason, CBS radio executives noted, "We also have strict standards and practices in place and have made clear our expectations in this area. We will not tolerate commentary that aims to demean, discriminate, or harass anyone in our listening audience." Although the executives were obviously aware of Carton's troubled past—the press release about Carton's first radio gig in Buffalo called the show "irreverent"—they were also aware, as the release went on to note, that the program swiftly became a ratings smash.

CHAPTER 2

How Right-Wing Radio Killed Immigration Reform

Conservative talk radio does deserve credit—or blame—for stopping that bill. It was one of the first times we actually played such a role, and I'm very proud of it. It was a real silent majority issue, taken up on the quintessential grassroots medium. —Mike Gallagher

The immigration debate was a classic example of how conservative talk radio was the only medium serving the public with information they weren't getting anywhere else. It was the finest hour of talk radio. —John Ziegler

On the afternoon of June 23, 2007, the Associated Press reported that "immigration has supplanted Iraq as the leading issue on television and radio talk shows, complicating the prospects of a Senate bill desperately wanted by President Bush."

The conservative radio talk shows in particular were having an especially great impact on the immigration debate, an impact which, the AP added, "reached new heights last week, with one host effectively writing an amendment for when the Senate returns to the imperiled bill this week."

The Secure Borders, Economic Opportunity and Immigration Reform Act of 2007, also known as the Comprehensive Immigration Reform Act of 2007, rose phoenixlike from the ashes of three previously failed bills. Senators John McCain and Ted Kennedy proposed the first in May 2005; Senators John Cornyn and Jon Kyl introduced the second in July of that same year, followed by Senator Arlen Specter in May 2006. The bipartisan group responsible for creating the 2007 bill was known as the Gang of 12 and included Senators Kennedy, Specter, McCain, Kyl, Lindsey Graham, and Mel Martinez among its members. The bill's sponsor was a Democrat, Senate Majority Leader Harry Reid.

The plan, which was strongly supported by President Bush, included a new "Z" visa that would allow illegal immigrants to remain permanently in the United States; a temporary guest worker "Y" visa that would require workers to go back to their native countries after two years; and a provision called the DREAM Act, which would open opportunities for young illegal immigrants either to attend college or join the military. But the bill met with fierce opposition from most conservative pundits, who felt that illegal immigrants should be treated as criminals who had violated U.S. laws and threatened national security. Their point of view, articulated early and often by prominent talk show hosts Rush Limbaugh, Sean Hannity, Bill O'Reilly, Michael Savage, and many other lesser stars in the talk show firmament, increased resistance to the bill from the public and in Congress.

Conservative radio hosts spent months denouncing the proposed legislation, which would have tightened borders and workplace enforcement, as well as created a guest worker program and provided ways of attaining legal status for many of the estimated

12 million illegal immigrants in the United States. In so doing, the right-wing talkers consistently reframed the complicated compromise reform measure as simply providing amnesty (or "shamnesty," as they dubbed it) for illegal immigrants. The bill's supporters on both sides of the aisle argued that the proposed legislation, however imperfect, was still better than any other politically practical alternative.

Fearing the bill's powerful bipartisan support in Congress and the White House, the radio talkers set out to challenge its political viability by ratcheting up their rhetoric. Rush Limbaugh warned on his nationally syndicated radio show that Mexican immigrants who illegally enter the United States are not only "poor and unwilling to work" but are "a renegade, potential criminal element." He made his remarks during a conversation with a caller about protests in Los Angeles against the bill, which would have criminalized providing aid to undocumented immigrants and laid stiff penalties on the many U.S. employers who hired them, defying Limbaugh's contention that illegal immigrants are "unwilling to work."

Michael Savage dubbed the new immigration bill the "I Bomb" and vowed to "derail this train of treason." In an e-mail to the right-wing Web site NewsMax.com, Savage wrote that our "culture [is] being destroyed by greed, greed, greed. Bush is the chief culprit. He's wanted this from day one. In fact, we played a sound bite yesterday of him gleefully looking forward to the Democrat-controlled new Congress last fall! At last he could push through his ultra-internationalist agenda." Senator John McCain, a chief proponent of the bill, "is now finished," Savage added. "I instructed my listeners to bombard Congress with millions of e-mails saying, 'No

Amnesty...We'll Vote You Out.' I reminded them [that] we stopped
the Dubai Ports Deal, and we have the voting power to stop Bush
from dropping the I Bomb on America." Savage was right in two
respects: Congress was bombarded by e-mails (and worse, as we
shall see below) from radio talk show listeners, and as a result of
the radio rebellion, America was spared the "I Bomb."

Meanwhile another top-rated talker, Bill O'Reilly, also busily
sounded the alarm. According to O'Reilly, supporters of the immigration bill "hate America, and they hate it because it's run primarily by white Christian men. Let me repeat that. America is run
primarily by white Christian men, and there is a segment of our
population who hates that, despises that power structure." O'Reilly
continued: "So they, under the guise of being compassionate, want
to flood the country with foreign nationals, unlimited, unlimited,
to change the complexion—pardon the pun—of America. Now,
that's hatred, too."

O'Reilly consistently claimed that the goal of pro-immigration
activists was to alter the racial demographics of the United States.
During the April 11, 2006, edition of his Fox News Channel cable
television talk show *The O'Reilly Factor*, for example, he declared,
"There is a movement in this country to wipe out 'white privilege'
and to have the browning of America." And during an interview
on his radio talk show *The Radio Factor* on the same day, he repeatedly tried to provoke a guest to acknowledge that he and other
advocates for immigrant rights were motivated by a desire to force
white Americans into the minority.

"These are hidden agendas," O'Reilly warned on *The Radio
Factor*. "The *New York Times* would never cop to that, ever, but if
you read consistently their editorials, they have no solution to bor-

der security. They don't want any sanctions on illegal aliens who come here and even commit crimes. They want criminal aliens to stay, and they don't want any sanctions on businesses who continue to hire illegal aliens even after the Z visa is issued."

Ever a demagogue, O'Reilly neglected to mention that leading conservative members of Congress had pushed for the immigration bill or that one of the most conservative American presidents in history strongly supported it. Instead, he blamed "liberals" and the *New York Times* for an "insane" bill that would result in the evaporation of the nation. "America disappears. That's where Pat Buchanan is right. You let that happen, there's no more United States of America. It's gone. You have United States of the World, because everybody comes here with no restrictions."

On June 7, the Senate tried three times without success to end discussion of the bill and move it toward passage. By the time it was brought back for discussion a few weeks later, the attacks against it had reached fever pitch. Still, there remained a chance in late June 2007 that a compromise, however painful, could be attained and a bill easing America's decades-old immigration dilemma would pass. After all, the full weight of President Bush and the White House was behind the proposed legislation, and many in Congress were supporting the administration, including leading members of the Republican Party—some of whom, the AP reported, "have defied the broadcast pundits." But other GOP lawmakers, the wire service noted, "have tried to placate them, even to the point of accepting their ideas for amendments."

Senator Jon Kyl, the Arizona Republican who was a key negotiator backing the bill, was nevertheless one of those placating lawmakers, going so far as to assure reporters that "we are trying to include" several ideas offered by talk radio host Hugh Hewitt in amendments to the bill. Hewitt, a conservative who had already criticized many aspects of the proposed legislation, invited Kyl to appear as a guest on his radio program and then demanded, "Does the bill provide for any separate treatment of aliens, illegal aliens from countries of special concern?" Kyl replied, "It's going to, as a result of your lobbying efforts to me."

Rather than attempt to pacify the pundits, however, some Republican senators favoring passage of the immigration bill decided to adopt a more confrontational approach. Senator Lindsey O. Graham of South Carolina, one of the bill's chief architects, archly observed that opponents of the deal were verging on racism. "We've been down this road before," Graham said on the ABC News program *This Week.* "No Catholics, no Jews, Irish need not apply."

But Republican pushback to the right-wing talkers often backfired, as Trent Lott of Mississippi (who as the Minority Whip held the Republican Party's number two Senate leadership position) soon discovered. Faced with the fervent opposition of Hugh Hewitt, Rush Limbaugh, and their fellow right-wing radio luminaries, Lott loudly proclaimed that some of them didn't even know what was in the voluminous bill. In frustration, he complained to reporters, "Talk radio is running America. We have to deal with that problem."

That problem had begun manifesting itself in potentially dangerous ways—such as in mail received by Senator Mel Martinez, Republican of Florida, himself an immigrant who had been a leading advocate of reform. As the *New York Times* reported, thousands of angry messages opposing the legislation flooded his offices, both in Washington and Florida—but what really concerned Martinez was a threatening letter he received at his home. Although he declined to elaborate on the nature of the threat, Martinez did turn the letter over to District of Columbia police. Later, mindful of the opprobrium visited on Lott for his remarks, Martinez joked, "I ain't saying a thing," when asked about the radio-generated response to the immigration bill. "When we want to be on talk radio, we find a way to get on, because we like their views and we like their audience," Martinez added more seriously. "So when we don't like their message, we ought to be willing to take the pain."

The threat sent to Martinez wasn't the only menacing message that senators received. Richard Burr, a North Carolina Republican who was undecided on the bill, said his office received a telephone call that "made a threat about knowing where I lived." Burr also passed the threat along to the authorities. "There were enough specifics to raise some alarm bells," he said. Lindsey Graham said he too had received threats in telephone calls and letters to his office, and that several other senators had told him privately that they also received similar messages. At least one e-mail sent to senators was also forwarded to the authorities. That e-mail concluded, in referring to supporters of the bill, "They need to be taken out by *any means.*"

"Nobody likes to talk about it, but a very small percentage of people involved in this debate really have made racial and bigoted remarks," Graham said. "The tone that we create around these debates, whether it be rhetoric in a union hall or rhetoric on talk radio, it can take people who are on the fence and push them over emotionally."

Certainly some callers to the talk radio shows had expressed their opposition to the immigration bill in threatening, racist terms. It remains unclear exactly who was behind the threats sent to the senators, or what truly inspired them. In any event, there is no doubt that, as the *Times* concluded, "At the heart of the opposition rest conservative hosts on talk radio and cable television, which often are a muscular if untamed piece of the Republican message machine."

That raw muscle was activated as never before by fear of the passage of the much-reviled "shamnesty" bill. Capitol Hill switchboards were deluged as thousands of talk radio listeners called members of Congress to register their dismay. The lines hadn't been so jammed by a single issue since the impeachment of President Bill Clinton. This time, however, it was Republicans (those supporting the bill, at least) who faced the most intense opposition; it was the first time they had ever felt the brunt of what the *Times* accurately termed "an advocacy machine built around conservative talk radio and cable television programs that have long buttressed Republican efforts to defeat Democrats and their policies." Senator John W. Warner, a Republican who had represented Virginia for 29 years, admitted he had never seen anything like it. "I've experienced all the events in that period of time," Warner said, "but this is clearly the high-water mark."

"I'm sure a lot of the people who have taken a high-profile position on this have been threatened, but what are you going to do?" Senator Graham asked. "One of the requirements of public service in modern America is dealing with a few voices that are full of hate. And our discourse and the way we politic, the way we engage each other, brings that out." Other senators were neither so forthright nor courageous, saying they did not care to be identified as speaking critically of the broadcasters out of fear of the same conservative backlash that befell senators Lott, Graham, and others.

Trent Lott's remarks in particular incensed the conservative talk show hosts, because they had supported him over the years, rallying to his defense in 2002, for example, when he came under fire for racially insensitive remarks that for a time cost him his party leadership post. Now, to Lott's apparent surprise, right-wing talkers came out swinging. Rush Limbaugh, generally considered to be *primus inter pares* among right-wing talkers, reacted angrily, saying on-air, "When I hear a United States senator say that what I do for a living is a 'problem' that the government has to 'deal with,' you can interpret it any number of ways. He's either saying, 'Well, we're going to have to come up with our own ways to overcome them,' or 'We're going to just have to wipe them out.'" Limbaugh then turned the tables on Lott, asking his audience, "What are *we* going to do about Mississippi senator Trent Lott?"

Michael Savage, host of *The Savage Nation*, accused Lott of dispatching Nazi storm troopers against his critics. The Atlanta-based talk show host Neal Boortz wrote on his Web site that Lott was "upset that the American people got right into the middle of the conversation over the problem with illegal aliens and it didn't turn out all that well for the pro-amnesty forces." Boortz caustically added, "If Trent Lott and his other buddies up on the Hill aren't listening to 'talk,' then what are they listening to? The answer is either their wallet or their legacy."

Of course, Democrats and progressives have long borne the brunt of tongue-lashings from conservative talk radio hosts. But by joining with their colleagues in attempting to come up with a bipartisan solution to America's immigration problem, Republican conservatives suddenly became targets of right-wing radio ire as well...and they didn't like the feeling.

"I've had my phones jammed for three weeks. Yesterday I had three people answering them continuously all day," Lott said. "To think that you're going to intimidate a senator or any senator into voting one way or the other by gorging your phones with phone calls...is not an effective tactic. But it's their right to do that."

Alabama Republican senator Jeff Sessions, who had been a frequent guest of conservative hosts discussing immigration, weighed in, telling reporters, "I can't imagine what Trent was thinking. Maybe his mouth was moving and his brain was in neutral." Sessions also hailed the role that talk radio played in the debate. "Talk radio was sort of the watchdog on this. Who else was watching out? Who else was reading the bill?" he asked. "I think people have learned more from talk radio than from reading the newspapers." Anxious to indicate that he at least had gotten the message from right-wing radio hosts and their enraged listeners, he added, "A decent respect for our constituents means when they have very serious problems with an important piece of legislation, perhaps we should back off."

The treatment of Lott, Graham, and other outspoken congressional supporters of the proposed immigration legislation contrasted sharply with that given to pundit-placating Jon Kyl and certainly to opponents of the bill. Hugh Hewitt, a prolific writer and blogger, in addition to being a talk radio host, used his Web site to hail Kyl as "perhaps the single most effective and principled conservative in the United States Senate."

In the end, of course, the right-wing radio hosts claimed their victory, and Republicans acknowledged their influence. Lindsay Mabry, a spokeswoman for Georgia Republican senator Saxby Chambliss (who shifted from supporting to opposing the bill), admitted, "Neal Boortz, he popped us pretty good." Mabry said Chambliss consulted with Neal Boortz on immigration, even though he had not even been an on-air guest of the talk show host during the debate. As Michael Harrison, editor and publisher of *Talkers*, put it, "Talk radio should be credited with possibly saving the American people from George Bush's immigration bill."

Kathleen Hall Jamieson of the University of Pennsylvania, a frequent commentator on the intersection of media and politics, later explained how it all works. "Talk radio and talk TV are most effective when there's an immediate action pending," she said. "It's a classic instance of mobilization with all the pieces in place." But one piece of the mobilization was different this time; *Republican* politicians were the ones whose ox was gored. "They always assumed they owned conservative talk radio," Harrison explained. "But support of conservatives by talk radio was only being borrowed as long as conservatives felt that Republicans served the conservative movement." Trent Lott summed it up by noting, "When they're with you, it's great. When they're not, it's not good."

Welcome to the club, progressives might say. For decades, liberals, Democrats, minorities, immigrants, homosexuals, women, and just about anyone not strongly identified with conservative or libertarian ideology have from time to time experienced the wrath of right-wing talk radio. But the talkers' response to Lott's assertion that they are "a problem" may have reflected the beginning of their broader disenchantment with the Republican Party itself.

Michael Harrison believes that the immigration debate may have foreshadowed future criticism of leading Republicans on other issues, ranging from tax policy to spending and even Iraq. When *Talkers* bestowed its 2007 Freedom of Speech Award on Michael Savage for his criticism of President Bush, it marked the first time, Harrison noted, the magazine had honored a radio show host for speaking out against someone of his own political persuasion.

In winning the battle against immigration reform, however, the right-wing talkers may have lost a much larger political war. It's been two decades since Congress last passed a major immigration bill, about the same amount of time since Rush Limbaugh first became a force over America's airwaves. During that period, the demographics of the United States has shifted dramatically, as has the makeup of the national Republican Party.

"In 1986, radio talkers like Limbaugh could not harness the power of millions of devoted daily listeners to bring national Republican political figures to heel, and the Hispanic vote share was negligible," Thomas Schaller noted in a post on Salon.com. "Twenty years later, Limbaugh is the most popular talk radio host in America, and there are millions of Spanish-speaking immigrants living alongside Rush's listeners in the kinds of red states where Spanish was rarely heard before. At the same time, the Latino vote has grown to 10 million. The GOP is now forced to choose between its reliable base of close-the-border, English-only cultural whites and the rapidly growing bloc of swing-voting Hispanics."

John McCain, the lone supporter of immigration reform among the 2008 Republican presidential candidates, bore as much of the brunt of the backlash as the hapless Trent Lott. During one congressional meeting on the bill, McCain insulted fellow

Republican senator John Cornyn, calling Cornyn's objections to the legislation "chickenshit"—doubtless a sign of the severe stress McCain was under. Later, on a conference call with a group of conservative bloggers, McCain also attacked fellow presidential hopeful and rival Mitt Romney for his inconstancy on the subject of immigration, saying caustically, "Maybe I should wait a couple weeks and see if [Romney's position] changes. Maybe he can get out his small varmint gun and drive those Guatemalans off his yard."

Presidential candidate Rudolph Giuliani also reacted to the pressure exerted by the talk show political pipers by changing his tune. The former mayor of New York had long supported greater rights for immigrants. (While mayor, Giuliani instructed New York City employees, including police officers, not to cooperate with federal immigration agents looking for illegal aliens.) When chasing Republican presidential primary votes, however, Giuliani tried to explain his position by saying the agents were wasting resources chasing "cooks and gardeners" and that he was afraid illegal immigrants wouldn't cooperate with police during criminal investigations for fear of being deported. Initially, candidate Giuliani's own immigration policy plan, which he liked to present in national security terms, was not very different from the compromise bill before Congress. The far right's response to this stance was epitomized by a cartoon image of a sombrero-wearing *bandito* with Giuliani's face superimposed on it that appeared on the Free Republic Web site with a caption reading, "Borders? Borders? We don' need no steenking borders!" Faced with such ardent opposition, Giuliani soon began moving away from his previously pro-immigrant positions.

During the right-wing radio-inspired immigration insurrection, numerous Republican presidential candidates, including

Giuliani, debated in New Hampshire. To his credit, John McCain continued to express support for the battered-but-still-breathing reform legislation. But Giuliani, whose views on the subject had been similar to McCain's in the past, called the bill "a typical Washington mess" that had "no real unifying purpose." Shortly thereafter, as a guest on Hugh Hewitt's radio program, Giuliani said that he thought the immigration problem could be solved without relying on new legislation. By late June, when the bill was before Congress, Giuliani had come full circle. The *New Yorker* noted, "Echoing the view of conservative broadcaster Sean Hannity, on whose show he has become a regular guest, Giuliani said he had become convinced that the U.S. government first had to demonstrate that "it could control the borders before taking up the question of eventual citizenship for illegals." But Giuliani was not the only Republican presidential hopeful to get the immigration message, as Schaller wrote. The "ever-elastic" Mitt Romney had already quickly positioned himself as McCain's "worst enemy on immigration," and Sam Brownback, another senatorial presidential wannabe who had originally cosponsored McCain's reform bill, later decided "to renounce Satan and recast himself as a nativist," as Schaller caustically phrased it.

Owing in large part to the intense rhetoric from the talk radio pundits, the Comprehensive Immigration Reform Act of 2007 was voted down and left for dead on June 28, 2007. The long-term effects of the internecine battle on the Republican Party are still unclear, but the victory clearly left the right-wing radio show hosts and their listeners ascendant, flexing their muscles and eagerly preparing for their next battle.

THE TOP TALK
RADIO AUDIENCES

(Weekly Monday-Sunday cume estimates 12-plus in millions rounded off to the nearest .25 million based upon *TALKERS* magazine's analysis of a national sampling of Arbitron reports supported by other reliable indicators in rated and non-rated markets based on Fall 2007.)

Radio Talk Show Host	Minimum Weekly Cume (millions)	Radio Talk Show Host	Minimum Weekly Cume (millions)
1. Rush Limbaugh	14.00+	10. Rusty Humphries	2.25+
2. Sean Hannity	13.00+	Kim Komando	
		Lars Larson	
3. Michael Savage	8.25+	Jim Rome	
Dr. Laura Schlessinger		11. Bob Brinker	1.75+
4. Glenn Beck	6.50+	Tom Leykis	
		Mancow	
5. Laura Ingraham	5.25+	12. Dr. Joy Browne	1.50+
Mark Levin		Alan Colmes	
6. Neal Boortz	4.25+	Thom Hartmann	
Dave Ramsey		Hugh Hewitt	
7. Mike Gallagher	4.00+	Lionel	
Michael Medved		G. Gordon Liddy	
		Dennis Miller	
8. Jim Bohannon	3.25+	Stephanie Miller	
Clark Howard		Randi Rhodes	
Bill O'Reilly		13. Dr. Dean Edell	1.00+
Doug Stephan		Bill Handel	
9. Bill Bennett	3.00+	Michael Reagan	
Jerry Doyle			
George Noory			
Ed Schultz			

The numbers in The Top Talk Radio Audiences are estimates of national Arbitron numbers gathered directly by station reports and information provided by Arbitron and other sources. These figures are rough projections based upon a significant sample and do not represent exact Arbitron or any other ratings service totals. The Top Talk Radio Audiences is published twice-yearly in Spring and Fall editions of *TALKERS* magazine. Please credit *TALKERS* magazine if reproduced or cited. © 2008 Talk Media, Inc.

CHAPTER 3

The Top Ten Worst Shock Jocks (Minus Imus)

Conservative talk radio is a bit like car chases and traffic accidents on the side of the road: you can't not look. —John Moyers

1. RUSH LIMBAUGH
Hail, Dittoheads!

They are the 13.5 million people who listen weekly to Rush Hudson Limbaugh III, the most popular radio talk show host in America. After Limbaugh told his callers to simply say "ditto" when they agreed with him, in time the legions of faithful became known as "dittoheads."

Their leader is a balding, cigar-chomping man in his mid-50s who over the past 30 years has weighed anywhere from 250 to 350 pounds. His voice is deep and blunt, and though he had a television show for a few years in the early 1990s, Limbaugh correctly insists he has a "face made for radio." He's the author of two best-selling books about the conservative lifestyle; he's been thrice married and thrice divorced. He's a member of the Radio Hall of Fame and the host of an annual Leukemia & Lymphoma Society fundraising telethon. In 2002 *Talkers* dubbed him the greatest radio talk show host of all time. And he's no stranger to controversy.

In October 2006 actor Michael J. Fox appeared in a televised campaign ad supporting Missouri Democratic senatorial hopeful Claire McCaskill's pro-stem-cell research position. Fox suffers from Parkinson's Disease, and signs of his affliction were evident to viewers of the ad. On his show later that week, Limbaugh claimed that Fox was exaggerating. "He's moving all around and shaking, and it's purely an act...This is really shameless of Michael J. Fox. Either he didn't take his medication or he's acting...This is the only time I've ever seen Michael J. Fox portray any of the symptoms of the disease he has." Dittoheads watching Limbaugh's show via his Internet "DittoCam" even saw the host mimic Fox's movements.

A public outcry ensued. Parkinson's experts declared Fox's symptoms to be genuine. "Any other interpretation is misinformed," neuroscientist Elaine Richman said. Limbaugh later apologized on radio and television and via his Web site but still tried to maintain an anti-Democrat foothold by asserting, "Michael J. Fox is allowing his illness to be exploited."

Another example: In 2003 the sports cable network ESPN added Limbaugh as a color analyst to its weekly football program *Sunday Night NFL Countdown.* After an ugly Philadelphia Eagles loss, Limbaugh remarked of Philadelphia quarterback Donovan McNabb, "Sorry to say this, I don't think he's been that good from the get-go. I think what we've had here is a little social concern in the NFL. The media has been very desirous that a black quarterback does well. There is a little hope invested in McNabb, and he got a lot of credit for the performance of this team that he didn't deserve." ESPN immediately released an official statement distancing itself from the remarks, and a few days later, after less than a month on the program, Limbaugh resigned while protesting that his remarks were aimed more at the mainstream media than at McNabb's skin color. ("Color analyst" indeed.)

A week after his *Countdown* resignation, Limbaugh confessed to his radio listeners that he was addicted to prescription pain medication. He claimed to have begun taking the drug OxyContin years earlier in order to ease back pain. After more than two years of investigation, the Palm Beach district attorney had Limbaugh arrested for "doctor shopping"—using multiple physicians to fill multiple prescriptions and even getting his housekeeper to fill prescriptions for him. The charges were eventually dropped on the condition that Limbaugh seek counseling. Today he claims that his body is clean, though his reputation no longer is. Several years prior, on his television show, Limbaugh had declared, "Too many whites are getting away with drug use...The answer is to go out and find the ones who are getting away with it, convict them, and send them up the river."

In addition to these controversies, in recent years Limbaugh has been battered by gradual hearing loss and continuing accusations by disaffected listeners and competitors of parroting a Republican Party line. But Limbaugh remains the leading talk radio host in the land. Who is he, and where did he come from?

A native of Cape Girardeau, Missouri, Limbaugh was born into a family of lawyers and judges, the son of parents who named him after a distant female relation. A truant childhood, followed by a brief radio stint under the name Rusty Sharpe, led to two semesters and a summer session at Southeast Missouri State, known as "Cape State" because so many locals attended it. Limbaugh failed nearly everything, even ballroom dancing, although he did receive an A in a course on American government. He earned a D in Speech 101, because, while he enjoyed public speaking, he refused to prepare notes and gave his presentations extemporaneously. Eventually he dropped out of school and left not only town but also the entire "Show Me" state. Limbaugh later told the *Southeast Missourian,* "For the next ten years of my life, everything I did was framed by 'I'll show them.'"

His first attempt to show them came in McKeesport, Pennsylvania, where Limbaugh worked as a disc jockey under the pseudonym Jeff Christie. Despite a Top 40 ranking, Limbaugh was fired for espousing his political views on-air; he then was hired and fired by two other stations, including one in Kansas City, after which he retreated to a public relations job for the Kansas City Royals baseball team for five years before trying again. After baseball he landed a job at KFBK in Sacramento. Following several more years of failure, he finally got it right. In 1988, four years after arriving in Sacramento, Limbaugh signed a syndication contract with EFM Media and quickly gained a national audience of 5 million. His numbers have grown ever since; the fact that his show airs from noon to three on weekdays, a time when most people are at work, makes his dominance of the airwaves all the more impressive.

Part of Limbaugh's appeal comes from his propensity for saying shocking and outlandish things ("more people have died at Chappaquiddick than have died in nuclear-power accidents"), but the reasons Limbaugh's program caught fire run much deeper than that. Limbaugh succeeds partly because he is a great public speaker, capable of delivering comic monologues on the fly, and also because his highly entertaining program is built around a cult of personality that makes listeners as interested in him as in the issues he discusses. As Ed McLaughlin, the former ABC Radio Networks president who first signed Limbaugh to syndication, said, "Radio is personality-driven," and the personality that Limbaugh puts forward is that of a fun-loving prankster who revels in his job. Limbaugh's show differs from most other talk radio shows, right- or left-leaning, in that it is, for the most part, guest-less, with only the occasional Bush family member, Republican bigwig, or right-associated entertainer (Sylvester Stallone, Jim Caviezel of *The Passion of the Christ*) brought in to break up the continuum of host monologues and call-in segments.

Limbaugh's sense of humor is the greatest reason for his success. He flew solo originally not only by refusing to add guests but also by mixing comedy and entertainment values with politics, something that was rare in an age of dour commentators. Limbaugh's show has used song parodies, often created by artist Paul Shanklin, ranging from a takeoff of "They're Coming to Take Me Away, Ha-Ha!" in order to describe Ross Perot in the early 1990s to "Barack, the Magic Negro," a "Puff, the Magic Dragon" spoof that posited Democratic presidential candidate Barack Obama's rise to be the result of white guilt. Limbaugh has uttered slang and catchy buzzwords that have entered the cultural lexicon, from "Senator Dick Turban" for Richard Durbin to "Gorbasm" for admiration of former Soviet leader Mikhail Gorbachev to "Club Gitmo" for the U.S. military prison at Guantanamo Bay.

He's also no stranger to attention-grabbing stunts, among the most famous of which have been Safe Talk, in which the host placed a condom over his microphone in order to protect listeners from hearing things that might offend them, and Caller Abortions, in which Limbaugh ended dissenting listeners' calls with the sounds of a vacuum cleaner and a woman screaming. Limbaugh advised squeamish listeners to think about how much worse real abortions were. Commenting on his personal brand of entertainment in a 1990 letter to the *New York Times*, Limbaugh said, "Critics insist that responsible discussions of great issues be tedious and formal...Enter talk radio, where people are free to participate in the dialogue by telling others what they think, rather than having to listen to the same endless parade of pointy heads and academics offered up by the morning shows, the midday shows, and the late shows on television." Talk radio, in other words, was made for his method, and vice versa.

Limbaugh's style has become so successful that at several points in his career he has been cast as a leading spokesman for the Republican Party. Limbaugh campaigned hard for George H.W. Bush during the 1992 presidential election, even inviting the president onto his show and in turn spending a night in the White House's Lincoln Bedroom. After Bush lost to Bill Clinton, Limbaugh pushed even harder for Republicans in the 1994 congressional elections, with "Operation Restore Democracy" helping to create a 54-seat swing from Democrats to Republicans. In the wake of the elections, he became so prominent that an attempt to revive the Fairness Doctrine, a dormant Federal Communications Commission policy that had once mandated balanced amounts of airtime for discussion of matters of public interest and concern, earned the Capitol Hill nickname of the "Hush Rush" bill.

Along with attempting to influence congressional elections and legislation, Limbaugh has also sought to define contemporary American conservatism, writing in a 2005 *Wall Street Journal* op-ed that conservatives "believe in individual liberty, limited government...welfare reform, faith-based initiatives, political speech, homeowner rights, and the war on terrorism. And at our core we embrace and celebrate the most magnificent governing document ever ratified by any nation—the U.S. Constitution."

Oftentimes, however, Limbaugh privileges style over substance. The Michael J. Fox dustup exemplifies the host's propensity for spouting misinformation, particularly in relation to science and medicine, which makes his catchphrase, "I'm not making this up, folks," more than slightly suspect. According to Limbaugh, nicotine is not addictive, cigarettes don't cause emphysema, and "we have more acreage of forest land in the United States today than we did at the time the Constitution was written."

Limbaugh has tried to discredit the environmental movement by calling its members "wackos" who "look at capitalism as an enemy of the people." Recently he has argued that carbon monoxide is not a toxic pollutant and that "Antarctica ice is actually increasing." The Environmental Defense Fund has even issued a pamphlet entitled "The Way Things Really Are," in which the Princeton University–employed authors argue that Limbaugh "allows his political bias to distort the truth about a whole range of important scientific issues."

Limbaugh has also distorted the truth in order to attack other liberal positions, with Bill and Hillary Clinton among his favorite targets. During the Clinton administration, he falsely claimed that Chelsea Clinton's Quaker private school had made her write an essay entitled "Why I Feel Guilty Being White," using a nonexistent CBS News story as his source. During the 2004 election season,

Limbaugh suggested that the Clintons secretly funded the Swift Boat Veterans for Truth group that distorted John Kerry's Vietnam War record. He has repeatedly attacked the Democrats as working against America's interests, claiming that liberals "will not defend the American military" and "will not defend freedom," and that "they hate this country."

The Donovan McNabb controversy illustrates a different Limbaugh tendency: Long before Don Imus ever mentioned "nappy-headed hos," Limbaugh frequently made African Americans the butt of his jokes. When he was starting out as a broadcaster in the 1970s, he once told a black caller, "Take that bone out of your nose, and call me back." Ten years later, after he had accepted a syndication deal, he openly wondered on the air, "Have you ever noticed how all composite pictures of wanted criminals resemble Jesse Jackson?" In response to a caller several years ago who argued that black voices needed to be heard more often, Limbaugh said, "They are 12 percent of the population. Who the hell cares?"

More than 15 years after the Rodney King riots and the Hill-Thomas hearings, Limbaugh is still racially offensive. Referring to the devastation in New Orleans, post–Hurricane Katrina, he said, "Once the whites leave town, all you've got is overwhelming lawlessness...it's a proven, demonstrable fact." The following February he said, "They oughta change Black History Month to Black Progress Month and start measuring it."

His insults aren't saved for African Americans alone; in referring to a racially segregated competition on the TV show *Survivor*, Limbaugh argued not only that the black team would have the worst swimmers but also that the Asian American group "probably will outsmart everybody," and that the Hispanic group would likely win, because Hispanics "have shown a remarkable ability to cross borders" and "they will do things other people won't do." Limbaugh recently equated legendary farm worker union organizer César Chávez with Venezuelan president Hugo Chávez and said, "Hugo, César, whatever. A Chávez is a Chávez. We've always had problems with them."

Women are are also frequent targets. Limbaugh popularized the term "feminazi," which he defines as a woman "to whom the most important thing in the world is that as many abortions as possible take place." He famously listed one of his "35 Undeniable Truths" as, "Feminism was established as to allow unattractive women easier access to the mainstream of society" and said on his radio show, "Some of these babes, I'm telling you, like the sexual harassment crowd. They're out there protesting what they actually wish would happen to them sometimes." Limbaugh's own attitude toward harassment can be inferred from a sign he once had posted on his office door that read, "Sexual harassment at this work station will not be reported. However...it will be graded!!!"

The prescription drug scandal is only the most egregious example of Limbaugh's hypocrisy. After repeating accusations that Hillary Clinton helped murder Vince Foster, Limbaugh said, "I don't know who's accusing her of murdering anybody." In 1993 he told those voting in congressional elections, "I have yet to encourage you people or urge you to call anybody," while a scant hour later he said, "The people in the states where these Democratic senators are up for reelection in '94 have to let their feelings be known...These senators, you let them know."

Limbaugh regularly accused Bill Clinton of being a Vietnam War draft dodger when his own draft history is murky; Limbaugh was declared 1-Y and medically unfit to serve because of a pilonidal cyst in his lower back and a "football knee." When the 1-Y classification was later eliminated, Limbaugh was retroactively reclassified as 4-F—but at the time Limbaugh was declared medically unfit for his "football knee," he wasn't 4-F, which was then reserved for more extreme medical issues. Yet on his radio show Limbaugh consistently told listeners only that he had been classified as 4-F, the more serious classification. Why fudge the facts?

Despite his faults, Limbaugh remains an industry giant, not only to listeners but also to fellow talk radio personalities across the political spectrum. In just 20 years he has moved from a fringe political player to an institutional figure, particularly on the right. But the main reason Limbaugh continues to hold a grip on the airwaves, even through his scandal-plagued times, is that he's a brilliant talker. His voice is funny, his manner is blunt, and several of his jokes will make you laugh with their sheer outrageousness even while you wince—or worse—in disagreement. For a great many of the aptly named dittoheads, the information and the opinions Limbaugh dispenses are one and the same. Whether that is good or bad is irrelevant, at least to his admirers; what matters now, as it mattered then, is that Rush Hudson Limbaugh III is very, very popular, and he is likely to remain so for a long time to come.

2. SEAN HANNITY
Lie, the Beloved Country

Sean Hannity's America is a great place to live. People are kind and responsible; parents care for their children; the government takes care of its decent, God-fearing citizens; and all those citizens obey the law. Words like "freedom," "justice," and "dignity" still have the original meanings the Founding Fathers assigned to them. And even though Sean Hannity's America no longer exists—indeed it never did—for four hours each weekday and an additional hour on the Lord's Day, the masses can listen to Hannity and maintain their faith in that halcyon, beloved, and entirely fictional country.

Hannity is the popular conservative half of the two-pronged Fox News Channel nightly talk show *Hannity & Colmes*, as well as the author of two books, the former sponsor of General Motors's "You're a Great American" giveaway campaign, the founder of the Republican dating site Hannidate, and the sole host of both the Fox News show *Sean Hannity's America* and the New York–based WABC radio show *The Sean Hannity Show*. As of this writing, Hannity is syndicated on more than 500 stations nationwide and, with more than 12.5 million weekly listeners, ranks second only to Rush Limbaugh among talk radio hosts.

A great portion of Hannity's talk radio audience arrives already familiar with the host from television, but that fact alone is insufficient to explain his popularity. The public package Hannity presents can be enormously appealing; unlike fellow conservative talker Michael Savage, who flaunts his "Doctor" title loudly and proudly, Hannity proffers the persona of the ordinary Joe. He is quick to cite his background as an Irish-Catholic bartender/carpenter-cum-college dropout before he landed on radio. Also unlike Savage, whose listeners can practically feel the spittle spewing from his mouth, Hannity never gets too worked up; he frequently engages his guests in animated debate, but he always proceeds calmly from what he believes to be logical positions. (A large billboard several years ago contrasted the two conservative talkers with the message "In with the old, out with the new," noting the rise in popularity the younger Hannity was then undergoing). In contrast to his friend the reedy-voiced conservative talker Mark Levin, Hannity has a deep, pleasing voice that soothes the ear.

The way in which Hannity typically treats his callers is also instructive; whereas Savage snubs them, O'Reilly chastises them, and Limbaugh mocks them, Hannity, of all popular conservative talk show hosts, is best at knocking down the professional wall that separates host from caller. He will not hesitate to refer to a caller as his friend, and at conversation's end—so long as he agrees with the person—he will often use his catchphrase, "You're a great American." A final reason for Hannity's popularity on radio may be the fact that he's extremely prominent on television, which lends his words more authority on radio—as with the other hybrid talkers like Glenn Beck and Bill O'Reilly—than they might otherwise carry.

How did Hannity come to this favored position? In 1987, in what has become a pattern throughout his career, Hannity was fired 40 hours into his first radio job for "discriminating against gays and lesbians," according to the *Independent*. In time (and, ironically, partly owing to an ACLU suit) the station offered to rehire him, but Hannity had already moved to Atlanta to fill the even more rabid talk show host Neal Boortz's old radio slot. In

1996, Fox News paired Hannity on a cable television program with the older, less telegenic, and allegedly liberal pundit Alan Colmes. Hannity proved so successful on television that a radio syndication deal soon followed. Colmes, who has been around longer, also has his own radio show, but it's always clear who dominates their shared airwaves.

How popular is Sean Hannity? Even though there are places where he is beaten consistently in head-to-head time slots—in Seattle, for instance, liberal radio talker Ed Schultz boasts ratings that regularly top Hannity's—the Hannity product is marketed to hundreds of outlets nationwide, while even the most popular liberal hosts are lucky to reach just dozens of stations.

The show has a fast-paced and entertaining production feel, and it's easy to see why programmers in many markets endorse it. The quality of Hannity's guests is consistently high, though their views are often one-sided. The show switches gears smoothly to make ample use of studio effects, with both guests and callers often accompanied by cartoon-style sound effects. Jill Vitale, a self-identified liberal who is Hannity's former producer and the current producer for moderate conservative talker John Gambling's radio show, says that Hannity's audience comprises New York City firefighters and police officers, Wall Street types, stay-at-home moms, traveling salesmen, and anyone who is "into protecting the country more."

Hannity's mass media formula, whether for radio, television, or print, is neatly posited in the introduction to his book *Let Freedom Ring: Winning the War of Liberty Over Liberalism*: "As Americans, we face two fundamental questions: First, are we truly prepared to fight this new war to wipe out terrorism and terrorist regimes, and win it decisively—no matter what sacrifices it requires or how long it takes? Second, are we once again prepared to teach our children the fundamental principles and values that make this country great—the values that make this country worth fighting for, living for, and dying for?"

These values are essentially in line with those of the greater conservative movement. In *Deliver Us from Evil: Defeating Terrorism, Despotism, and Liberalism,* Hannity uses the word "evil" 154 times to describe people and institutions as varied as Osama bin Laden, Jimmy Carter, and the entire United Nations. He frequently blames the "mainstream media" for corrupting and misguiding the American people. Although liberal media watchdogs like FAIR (Fairness and Accuracy in Reporting) and Media Matters for America have criticized him in the past, the media he attacks so consistently and vociferously have for the most part stayed curiously silent. On his radio show, he has said, "They [the media] are fat, they are lazy, they have a pack mentality, they are partisan, and they are not doing their job, and they are not doing a service for the American people, and they are failing in their mission, and they purposely fail in their mission, and they get away with it each and every day." In his condemnation, Hannity implicitly frames himself as an outsider, a rebel—someone who will bring the American people the unvarnished truth.

In point of fact, Hannity spouts mind-boggling amounts of misinformation. Arguably the most infamous example is his oft-quoted remark, "It doesn't say anywhere in the Constitution this idea of the separation of church and state." He has also suggested that the Democratic National Convention doctored the photos of Abu Ghraib prisoners in Iraq, and he fabricated a poll in order to claim that minorities supported Social Security. Senator John Kerry was one of Hannity's favorite targets during the 2004 presidential election campaign; for instance, Hannity claimed there was "an absence of evidence" that the Democratic presidential candidate had been in combat in the Vietnam War. Amazingly, he even went so far as to invite one of the members of the Swift Boat Veterans for Truth Committee onto *Hannity & Colmes* to commiserate with his guest over how *Kerry* had smeared the Swift Boaters. While narrating the official welcoming video for the 2004 Republican National Convention, Hannity cited several alleged Kerry votes in the Senate for cutting the budgets for American intelligence and weaponry—votes that had never been cast.

Hannity's approach is not mere mendacity, however. To listen to him at work is to observe a master class in meticulously crafted, consistently employed propaganda. There is a long record of right-leaning bias on *Hannity & Colmes*; while the clearly conservative Hannity proudly asserts his positions, his supposedly equal though obviously weaker liberal cohost, Alan Colmes, often acquiesces in order to avoid argument. Although the show's producers preach a "fair and balanced" discussion between the cohosts (even using a stopwatch to ensure they get equal amounts of speaking time), the majority of the show's guests tend to be conservative, as do the majority of the viewpoints. (In response to the Limbaugh drug abuse scandal, Colmes said on the air, "We in talk radio owe Rush a debt of gratitude, no matter what side we're on.")

Hannity's America, the weekly Fox News TV talk show he has hosted since January 2007 in addition to *Hannity & Colmes*, goes even further, unfettered by any cumbersome need to nod in the direction of liberal viewpoints. Hannity commonly introduces conservative guests as coming from the "good side" and presents a segment called "Your America" about low and degrading things done by liberals. He tends to win arguments not through facts and reason but by doggedly repeating points until his guests are overwhelmed.

Producer Jill Vitale says Hannity relishes debate. "There have been crazy debates where guests have hung up," Vitale told us. "But Sean expects that." Although Hannity is not a screamer, he has no qualms about strongly asserting his opinions, telling Democrats in October 2006, "I want you to stay home on Election Day. Your vote doesn't matter anyway." He often wins arguments by putting guests on the spot with an absurd question like: "Is it that you hate this president or that you hate America?" or "Governor, why wouldn't anyone want to say the Pledge of Allegiance, unless they detested their own country or were ignorant of its greatness?" And when all else fails, Hannity (like O'Reilly) will assert his point of view simply by silencing his opponent; one FAIR study found that Hannity frequently turns off the microphone of guests he disagrees with.

Hannity has certainly made his share of controversial statements; part of the reason he was fired from his first radio job was for saying, "Anyone listening to this show that believes homosexuality is a normal lifestyle has been brainwashed. It's very dangerous if we start accepting lower and lower forms of behavior as the normal." And between 1997 and 1999 Hannity regularly accused Haitian immigrant Abner Louima, who had been forcibly sodomized by a New York Police Department officer while in custody, of trying to cover up a "gay sex act." The officer later confessed to the crime.

That said, Hannity tends to leave the truly explosive comments to his more extreme guests like Pat Buchanan, Oliver North, or Ann Coulter (with whom Hannity sympathized against the public outcry over her use of the word "faggot" to describe Democratic presidential candidate John Edwards). Nor has Hannity, a father of two who has been married to the same woman since 1993, experienced any personal scandals akin to those that have afflicted Rush Limbaugh. It takes a carefully controlled personality to stage such carefully controlled positions.

With Hannity, what you see and hear seems to be what you get. Unlike talk show hosts O'Reilly, Savage, and Beck, who have all been by turns unreliable and irrational, Hannity remains remarkably consistent. Perhaps more than any other conservative talk radio figure, the man's private and public personalities appear to be one and the same.

Hannity's goal is to stake out positions with little room for subtlety, nuance, or even humor. "You could go a year and never hear a joke," says *New Yorker* editor and short-story writer Ben Greenman, a devoted listener. Vitale agrees, saying the biggest difference between Hannity's on- and off-air personalities is that "people don't really get to hear the fun side of him on the air." Indeed, the image of the man who once teasingly gave Vitale a live lobster—knowing she was an animal rights activist—contrasts sharply with the man who said earnestly, "I'll tell you who should be tortured and killed at Guantanamo: every filthy Democrat in the U.S. Congress."

Listener Greenman and producer Vitale disagree about whether Hannity's program has the power to change minds. Greenman says, "I don't think it could ever change anybody's mind. The only thing that it could ever change would be the clock." Vitale counters, "People call all the time and say, 'I used to disagree with you, but I've listened to you and now I agree.'" Hannity took pride in helping to defeat the immigration bill through campaigns across his various media outlets, and his success suggests that he indeed influences public opinion. When enough people listen, a strong contingent can be led to believe—no matter what.

So Hannity continues to make erroneous and fact-free claims on-air, ranging from Iraq's supposed possession of nuclear weapons to Hillary Clinton having murdered Vince Foster to the conclusion that, aside from the Iraq war controversy, George W. Bush's presidency has been triumphant. But why let the facts get in the way of a good show? For three hours daily on the radio and another hour at night on cable television, Sean Hannity comes prepared, works hard, and is by most accounts excellent at his job as an entertainer. That's precisely the problem.

3. MICHAEL SAVAGE
One Nation, Under Many Savages

Who is Michael Savage? On its surface the question seems obvious: he's a 66-year-old nationally syndicated conservative talk radio host whose program, *The Savage Nation,* airs five days a week from its home base of KNEW in San Francisco. He's the founder of the Paul Revere Society, which, according to its mission statement, aims to "take back our borders, our language, and our traditional culture from the liberal left corroding our great nation." He's a former MSNBC cable television talk host who was fired after four months on the job after he told a phone caller, "You should only get AIDS and die, you pig." He's also the third most popular radio talk show host in America, whose weekly audience of more than eight million listeners is surpassed only by Limbaugh and Hannity.

Dig deeper, however, and the question of who Savage is, and *how truly savage* he is, becomes far more complicated. "Savage" isn't his real name; it seems to speak to his heightened sense of masculinity, his aggression, and his antipathy toward minorities. Born Michael Alan Weiner, "Savage" is the child of Russian-Jewish immigrants. He earned two master's degrees and a Ph.D. in nutritional ethnomedicine from that liberal bastion the University of California, Berkeley. He's written two dozen books, five as Michael Savage and an additional 19 under his given name, on medicine, the subjects of which range from maintaining a healthy diet to breaking a cocaine habit. But by any name, he professes to know what's good for you.

Before the vitriolic monologist emerged, there was another, kinder and gentler Michael. This one roamed Greenwich Village and the Bay Area in the early 1970s, kept a weathered copy of *On the Road* in his back pocket, and lay on the beach with the renowned beat poets Allen Ginsberg and Lawrence Ferlinghetti whenever he wasn't working on stand-up comedy routines. He guarded Timothy Leary's LSD supply, and he even once posed naked in a photograph with Ginsberg, a well-known and very public homosexual, which he distributed among friends in an attempt to prove himself part of the counterculture. At some point, however, more than 25 years ago, something took a sinister turn and, like Prince Hal rejecting Falstaff, Savage suddenly disavowed his former friends. In a 2006 interview for *SF Weekly*, Savage explained, "I was once a child; I am now a man." In the same interview, he said of Ginsberg, "I looked at him almost like a rabbinic figure. Little did I know that he was the fucking devil." For Savage, rejecting his old friends was simply a part of growing up.

The moralist, the healer, and the hedonist—there's a tension between his three identities, which interact like a trio of siblings elbowing each other for seconds at the dinner table. As one listens to his conservative radio talk personality, one is moved to question whether it's his true self, not because Savage isn't consistent in his views, but because the views are so grotesque it's difficult to believe that *anyone*—let alone a former beatnik—could espouse them with a straight face. While it's more than passing strange for a homophobic, conservative radio host to work out of San Francisco, Savage continues to broadcast nationally from his base in the city he likes to call "San Fran Sicko."

Savage is so extreme that even many of his fellow right-wing talk radio personalities don't like him. Bill O'Reilly calls him a "smear merchant," while Neal Boortz refers to Savage as "the

Antichrist." Although *Talkers Magazine* recently bestowed its annual Freedom of Speech award upon Savage, publisher Michael Harrison says he thinks the man is "an asshole." Liberal advocacy organizations such as GLAAD and ACLU have censured him. Liberal media watchdog groups have compiled long lists of the especially inflammatory remarks Savage has made—many of which must be heard or seen in print to be believed. Collectively they justify the cautionary statement that is read by an announcer before each edition of *The Savage Nation.*

Why do so many different people dislike Savage and his *Nation*? Perhaps it's because Savage dislikes so many different people. In his book *The Savage Nation: Saving America from the Liberal Assault on Our Borders, Language and Culture*, he writes, "I was raised on neglect, anger, and hate. I was raised the old-fashioned way." Despite claiming to have originated the term "compassionate conservative" (and threatening to sue George W. Bush for appropriating it), Savage is usually far more passionate than compassionate.

On the issue of illegal immigration, he said:

> "We, the people, are being displaced by the people of Mexico. This is an invasion by any other name. Everybody with a brain understands that. Everybody who understands reality understands we are being pushed out of our own country."

On CNN news anchors:

> "Wolf Blitzer, a Jew who was born in Israel, [is] probably the most despicable man in the media next to Larry King, who

takes a close runner-up by the hair of a nose. The two of them together look like the type that would have pushed Jewish children into the oven to stay alive one more day to entertain the Nazis."

On homosexuality:

"The radical homosexual agenda will not stop until religion is outlawed in this country. Make no mistake about it. They're all not nice decorators…They threaten your very survival…Gay marriage is just the tip of the iceberg. They want full and total subjugation of this society to their agenda."

And in conclusion:

"Why should we have constant sympathy for people who are freaks in every society? I'm sick and tired of the whole country begging, bending over backwards for the junkie, the freak, the pervert, the illegal immigrant. All of them are better than everybody else. Sick."

Listening to a host for whom even George W. Bush is too liberal (Savage particularly lambastes the president on immigration issues) can be an intense experience. Yet millions of people do it. As *New Yorker* editor Ben Greenman says, "People who listen to Savage say that he's a little extreme but that some of the things he says are also true. I think his show does encourage you to think for yourself, because he's so weirdly contradictory."

Savage's three-hour program often consists of apoplectic rants—usually against a particular group or groups of people allegedly doing damage to America—that end with an animalistic, *Network*-like cry of "I can't take this anymore!" During calmer times, Savage ends his monologues with a huffy "That's just the way I see it." Sometimes Savage exhibits a rare and startling tenderness, for instance in his fond recollections of the film director Elia Kazan (famous not only for *On the Waterfront* but also for naming names to the House Un-American Activities Committee). And every so often Savage changes the subject, mentioning a great barber he's been to recently or a good movie he's just seen. There is something almost hypnotic about the up-and-down anger on the program; even though Savage's views are not always internally coherent, he is supremely confident and comfortable in expressing them. His ability to steer the course without having to resort to logic to support his points is a trait more often seen in politicians than commentators. Indeed, Savage briefly (if laughably) mulled a run for the 2008 presidency on the grounds that since neither the Democrats nor the Republicans were to be trusted, a nonpolitician like him might be exactly what the country needed.

Savage's main sources of anger these days are illegal immigrants, Islamic terrorists (a near-redundancy for him), and homosexuals. Unlike his parents, who legally emigrated to the United States, arriving in Ellis Island, illegal immigrants assault fundamental American values—or so Savage claims. They not only compromise the security of the border and bring drugs, crime, and disease with them, but they threaten the American way of life—or at least the white male way of life. In reference to Arabs, Savage has said that the "racist, fascist bigots" should be converted to Christianity because "Christianity has been one of the great salvations on planet Earth...It's the only thing that can probably turn them into human beings."

The shift in Savage's attitudes toward homosexuality may be the most revealing of his complex persona. When he was younger, his father mocked Savage's sexuality. "Michael would have on tight black jeans and a boat-necked sweater, and his dad would say, 'I don't like the way you're dressed. You look like a fag,'" childhood friend Alan Zaitz has said. In his first and only novel, *Vital Signs*, the protagonist (a fortyish Jew named Samuel Trueblood who shares many of Savage's biographical details) says, "I choose to override my desires for men when they swell in me, waiting out the passions like a storm, below decks." There are Savage's years with Ginsberg and Ferlinghetti, including a note to Ginsberg that read, "Watched a tourist from New Zealand taking pictures of Fijian people in the marketplace [and] thought of inserting my camera's lens in your A-hole to photograph the walls of your rectum." These days, his attitude is outright hostility, with, for instance, his continual assertion of a "homosexual mafia" trying to control the state of world affairs. Savage has also said that gay parenting is "child abuse" and that the sight of a gay couple "makes me want to puke."

In an interview with the right-wing Web site NewsMax.com, Savage said, "I guess people love my show because of my hard edge combined with humor and education. Those who listen to me say they hear a bit of Plato, Henry Miller, Jack Kerouac, Moses, Jesus, and Frankenstein." Frankenstein aside, that's not bad company, and hyperbole notwithstanding, there are still many members of the conservative faith who swear by him. He has been married to the same woman for 40 years and has two children, a daughter, who is a teacher, and a son, who is the creator of the RockStar Energy Drink. His wild popularity allows him to make increasingly outrageous statements: Victims of the 2004 Indian Ocean tsunami deserved the devastation because they were harboring terrorists; Democratic presidential candidate Senator Barack Obama was trained in a madrassa. One consistent quality of Savage's vitriol is that he spares no one he feels is contributing to the problem. The Republican Party and the Catholic Church, both of which wanted to help illegal aliens, were equally subject to his wrath.

Over and over again, one wonders where Savage's interest lies, why he is so angry and why he seems to take it all so personally. "It really is a mystery. I have no idea what happened to Michael Weiner," says Lawrence Ferlinghetti, whom Savage has gleefully denounced after his Bay Area days as the owner of "that once-famous communist bookstore," City Lights. "We were his friends, and as far as I know, we never did anything to him."

4. BILL O'REILLY
The Unfairest of Them All?

Oh, shut up! At this point, that's about all one can say about—or to—Bill O'Reilly. With a syndicated radio program that draws more than 3.25 million listeners on 400 stations, a top-rated cable "news" show on the Fox News Channel that boasts an average nightly audience of 2 million, multiple best-selling books and a syndicated newspaper column, and a sideline as an in-demand and highly compensated public speaker, O'Reilly can rightly proclaim that, in the course of one decade, he has become one of America's most popular, prolix, and powerful talkers.

But what is O'Reilly talking about? And what does he have to say for himself? In the course of researching this book, we attempted to speak directly with O'Reilly, but he claimed to be too busy talking to talk, and his handlers eventually informed me that he would "pass at this time." Perhaps it's just as well—talking to Bill O'Reilly is usually a one-way conversation, as numerous visitors to his talk shows can attest. As Marvin Kitman wrote in his O'Reilly biography, *The Man Who Would Not Shut Up*, "Having a conversation with Bill O'Reilly is like trying to take a drink from an open fire hydrant."

When two researchers from the Indiana University School of Journalism tallied O'Reilly's on-air use of seven rhetorical techniques commonly identified as elements of propaganda, they found that insulting epithets came out of the Big Talker's mouth at the astonishing rate of 6.88 times per minute. "It's obvious he's very big into calling people names, and he's very big into glittering generalities," said researcher Mike Conway. Fellow researcher

Maria Elizabeth Grabe added, "If one digs further into O'Reilly's rhetoric, it becomes clear that he sets up a pretty simplistic battle between good and evil. Our analysis points to very specific groups and people presented as good and evil."

His Manichean worldview, cocksure demeanor, and attack mode manners make O'Reilly one of the most polarizing figures in the volatile world of talk media. To conservatives, he's an icon—"the beloved voice of reason, a font of wisdom, a man who provides diversity on the airwaves," as biographer Kitman (a self-described liberal) puts it. To his many enemies, O'Reilly is "the most unfair and unbalanced of them all." But like him or not—and Kitman actually admits to liking him—there is little doubt that he is "unarguably the most loved and loathed media voice of the 21st century," as Kitman says.

Born in 1949 in the Washington Heights neighborhood of Manhattan, O'Reilly and his family soon moved to the suburbs of Long Island. He claims to have grown up in Levittown, New York's archetypal postwar working-class housing community, but, as with many of his claims, this one is not quite true; his home was actually located in a more well-to-do area. By all accounts, including his own, his life was shaped by his domineering father, an accountant with a big oil company. (Although O'Reilly consistently paints himself as a blue-collar everyman who had to fight for every break, his white-collar father was paid a very middle-class annual salary of $35,000, equivalent to close to $100,000 in today's dollars.) O'Reilly attended Chaminade High School, a strict Catholic academy for boys, which I also attended. At the time, he was widely regarded as a feisty, pompous, self-important jerk—qualities that served him well in his subsequent career as a feisty, pompous, self-important broadcaster.

After graduating from Marist College in Poughkeepsie, O'Reilly heeded his father's wishes and became an English teacher, but he quit after two years to obtain a master's degree in broadcast journalism from Boston University's College of Communication. While there, according to Jacob Heilbrunn, in a *New York Times* review of Kitman's biography and O'Reilly's own book, *Culture Warrior*, "He hustled to write as many controversial pieces as he could, denouncing the left-wing professor Howard Zinn as more interested in activism than in teaching his courses."

By 1975, O'Reilly had secured his first job in television at a small station in Scranton, Pennsylvania. His chosen persona was that of the idealistic "action reporter" who championed the little guy against the powerful interests. He bounced around several local television stations in larger markets such as Dallas and Denver, winning a local Emmy along the way and getting fired as often as he was hired. Finally, by 1980, he made his way back to New York, the biggest media market in the country, working first for the local CBS station and then for the network itself as a correspondent. But O'Reilly's restless nature soon prevailed. After the CBS Evening News cut him out of footage on his reporting of the 1982 Falkland Islands war, he left the network. By the mid-'80s he was back in local television and back in Boston, where once again our paths crossed.

I was working as a producer at the ABC affiliate WCVB when then news director Philip S. Balboni hired O'Reilly as a reporter and news commentator. Although he got along well with Balboni and others in management (an improvement over his days in

Dallas, Denver, and New York), the rest of us couldn't stand him. "He desperately annoyed people," Emily Rooney, who was then the assistant news director, told Kitman. "He upset the newsroom," agreed Balboni. "He was a discordant note." Although O'Reilly's abrasive personality and unbridled egomania were partly to blame, what distressed O'Reilly's coworkers most were his commentaries. Unusual at the time, when objectivity was a supposed hallmark of professional journalism, O'Reilly's highly opinionated commentaries offered more than a hint of what was to come. Kitman calls this period in O'Reilly's career "the true start of the man who wouldn't shut up."

Following abbreviated postgraduate study at Harvard's Kennedy School of Government, O'Reilly became a correspondent for ABC News, appearing on such programs as *World News Tonight, Good Morning America,* and *Nightline.* He left to join the syndicated tabloid television newsmagazine *Inside Edition,* where he quickly became the program's lead anchor, bringing what he termed his "Long Island edge" to the previously failing show. Soon he was a successful anchorman earning a million dollars a year, but in 1995 he temporarily left his career to return to Harvard to complete his master's in public administration. When Roger Ailes, head of the cable start-up Fox News Channel, hired O'Reilly to host his own show, his star ascended. *The O'Reilly Report* soon became *The O'Reilly Factor,* and in the highly competitive partisan world of 24/7 cable news, its ratings entered the stratosphere. Bill O'Reilly became a household name and a seemingly ubiquitous presence on America's airwaves and bestseller lists.

At first, according to *New Yorker* staff writer and Columbia Graduate School of Journalism dean Nicholas Lemann, O'Reilly "seemed to be a recognizable member of the conservative-talk-show-host species...he attacked Bill Clinton and Al Gore relentlessly; the Monica Lewinsky scandal was his signature subject." But today, a decade later, Lemann says (and a surprising number of O'Reilly's fellow right-wing talkers agree) that "O'Reilly has been playing O'Reilly so successfully for so long and has developed such a substantial library of hooks, tics, and subplots, that he sometimes seems to be parodying himself."

With his wide range of nutty complaints, O'Reilly comes off as not only delusional but increasingly deranged. His list of enemies is growing longer, and his attacks are becoming more disturbing. In recent years, he has:

- Threatened audience members who mention the name of his cable television rival Keith Olbermann with "a little visit" from "Fox security."
- Equated the liberal Daily Kos Web site with Nazis and the Ku Klux Klan.
- Identified the *New York Times* with "the far-left" and told Senator John McCain that both "want to break down the white Christian male power structure of which you're a part, and so am I, and they want to bring in millions of foreign nationals to basically break down the structure that we have."
- Fumed about a "War on Christmas," which he claims is part of a "secular progressive agenda" aimed at the passage of "programs like legalization of narcotics, euthanasia, abortion at will, gay marriage."

- Claimed that a Missouri boy who had been kidnapped and held captive for four years must have "liked...his circumstances" and could have escaped if he wanted to. He later said publicly he would apologize if proven wrong but has yet to do so, even after the boy's kidnapper was charged with multiple counts of rape and distributing child pornography.
- Denounced the progressive political advocacy group MoveOn.org as "the most vicious element in our society today" and called its employees "assassins."
- Assaulted a campaign aide for Senator Barack Obama when the man prevented him from asking Obama a question.

Such absurdity is nothing new on *The Fear Factor*, as some opponents have come to call O'Reilly's talk programs. Since its creation in 2004, the watchdog group Media Matters for America has regularly monitored O'Reilly's work. "Of all the news anchors, columnists, pundits, and reporters whose work we've critiqued and corrected, one stands above all the rest," Media Matters announced when bestowing its first annual "Misinformer of the Year" award on O'Reilly that year, noting "at least 75 (we stopped counting) lies, distortions, and mischaracterizations."

But O'Reilly's false and misleading claims didn't end after Media Matters first exposed them. In November 2005, one of his producers sneaked into an undergraduate-wide party sponsored by Brown University's Queer Alliance and filmed students without their knowledge or permission. O'Reilly later broadcast the footage, falsely claiming that the students had taken the illegal drug Ecstasy. He said, "These pinheads up at Brown, they are a very liberal administration. Liberal administrators do not make judgments about behavior. Therefore any and all behavior that stops short of violence is permissible on many college campuses...You would have been safer in Baghdad than on the campus of Brown University."

O'Reilly and his supporters like to maintain that he is ideologically unclassifiable, a populist who stands up for the little guy. They cite as evidence his "less than completely worshipful" attitude toward President George W. Bush. In his 2003 book *Who's Looking Out for You?* O'Reilly wrote, "Summing up, I believe George W. Bush is personally honest but is also a charter member of the power establishment club that plays by its own rules." As proof of his independence, he points to his few "liberal" positions—he's against the death penalty, favors gay civil unions and some degree of gun control, and is not entirely antiabortion. He says he has little in common with libertarians, except that he agrees taxes are too high.

But the really interesting question, as reviewer Jacob Heilbrunn asked, is "How did he do it? How did O'Reilly, an unemployed has-been only a decade ago, turn himself into a moneymaking empire... [and] a Fox News contract said to be in the neighborhood of $50 million?" Although Heilbrunn perversely finds O'Reilly a "potent (and welcome) antidote to the pap served up for decades by the television industry," Marvin Kitman, who conducted 29 interviews with O'Reilly while writing his biography, is perhaps a better source on the subject. He concluded that "O'Reilly's struggle isn't about conservative ideas. It's about parading his seething personal resentments in order to become the very thing he purports to despise: a celebrity."

This insight may lie at the heart of the disdain that many of O'Reilly's apparent fellow travelers express when asked about him. Conservative talker John Ziegler of California's top-rated KFI radio station calls O'Reilly "essentially a fraud." While many other conservative talk show hosts, from "Grand Poobah" Rush Limbaugh to major players Sean Hannity and Laura Ingraham to an aspirant like Ziegler, at least *seem* to believe in the philosophies they espouse on the airwaves, Bill O'Reilly at times seems to believe in little besides himself.

Misinformer of the Year: O'Reilly's Most Misleading Claims of 2004
(Source: Media Matters for America)

1. Bush did not oppose the 9/11 Commission.

O'Reilly defended President George W. Bush against a Kerry-Edwards '04 TV ad highlighting Bush's opposition to creation of the 9/11 Commission by denying that Bush had ever opposed the commission. In fact, Bush did oppose the creation of the 9/11 Commission.

2. Iraq possessed ricin, a powerful toxin.

In fact, the Duelfer Report (the final report of the Iraq Survey Group, led by Charles A. Duelfer, which conducted the search for weapons in Iraq following the U.S.-led invasion) indicates that Iraq did not have ricin.

3. Iraq had links to Al Qaeda.

O'Reilly claimed that terrorist Abu Musab al-Zarqawi constituted a direct link between Al Qaeda and Saddam Hussein's Iraq and then interrupted a former Clinton administration official who tried to correct him. He allowed a conservative guest to repeat without challenge other discredited claims about Iraq's supposed involvement in terrorism—claims O'Reilly himself had cited previously.

4. Made up a source.

O'Reilly fabricated a publication as a source for the putative success of an O'Reilly-advocated American boycott of French imports, claiming, "They've lost billions of dollars in France, according to the *Paris Business Review.*" Media Matters for America found no evidence for the existence of the publication.

5. Cited phony statistics.

While arguing that taxes on the rich are excessive, O'Reilly tried to invalidate the argument that wealthy Americans ought to pay more taxes by referring to false statistics about the tax burden the rich currently bear.

6. Doctored quotes.

During a continuing smear campaign against progressive financier, philanthropist, and political activist George Soros, O'Reilly doctored a 1995 quotation by Soros to make it seem as if Soros wished his own father dead.

7. Selective ignorance.

O'Reilly teased an upcoming segment of *The O'Reilly Factor*, broadcast live from the Democratic National Convention, by saying of convention speaker Senator Edward Kennedy: "When we come back, we'll let you listen to Ted Kennedy for a while, if he shows up." In fact, Kennedy was present and had been speaking for several minutes behind him, as O'Reilly could have easily seen.

8. Invented facts.

In a discussion about what went wrong for Democrats in the 2004 election, O'Reilly claimed they "lost votes from four years ago," that "18- to 24[-year-old]s didn't go" to the polls, and that "[c]ommitted Republicans didn't carry the day for the president, independents did." All three claims were false.

9. Lied outright.

O'Reilly lied three times during one radio broadcast in July 2004. Lie Number One: Bush tax cuts didn't create the budget deficit. Lie Number Two: "Socialistic" French, German, and Canadian governments tax at 80 percent. Lie Number Three: Canadian, British, and French media are "government-controlled," but Italian media is free.

10. Made extreme comparisons.

On June 10, 2004, in response to the release of Michael Moore's *Fahrenheit 9/11*, O'Reilly said that people who supported the movie were akin to those who supported Joseph Goebbel's films about Poland invading the Third Reich. He then compared Moore to Leni Riefenstahl and Al Franken to Goebbels.

5. GLENN BECK
The Sick Freak Show

Glenn Beck is one of the few personalities in conservative talk radio today who can provide full production value solely with his voice. On a given day *The Glenn Beck Program*'s 5 million-plus listeners hear a cavalcade of wacky sound effects, courtesy of the show's eccentric, energetic, and truly conservative host, who lovingly (and perhaps accurately) refers to his fans as "sick freaks."

The program's goofy irrationality is superseded only by its jarring pacing. Gag lines tumble over each other as if in an absurdist kaleidoscope; the show is less farce and more vaudeville, less Lubitsch and more *Airplane!* For those who can't get enough of the 44-year-old Beck on radio, he's also the host of "Glenn Beck on CNN Headline News," a correspondent on "Good Morning America," the author of two books, and a stand-up comic-cum-motivational speaker with two annual tours. Somehow the self-styled human cartoon had gained enough legitimacy by 2003 to host a series of well-populated rallies called "Glenn Beck's Rally for America" to support troops in Iraq.

A Yale dropout and recovering drug addict and alcoholic who converted to Mormonism, Beck airs on 230 stations and now ranks fourth in national talk radio audiences—but that's not counting those who tune in to his segments on CNN, where he appears three times nightly, first at 7:00 ET and then at 9:00 and again at midnight as a repeat. And while Beck has certainly said some oddball things on radio, it is television that has seen his most famous moments. Although CNN Headline News president Ken Jautz has said that "Glenn's style is self-deprecating, cordial...it's conversational, not confrontational," a brief look back reveals that it's hardly civilized.

*Some of my best friends are Muslims, but...*On November 14, 2006, Beck invited Representative-elect Keith Ellison, a Minnesota Democrat and the first Muslim ever elected to the United States Congress, onto his show. After asking, "May we have five minutes here where we're just politically incorrect and I play the cards face up on the table?" Beck said, "OK. No offense, and I know Muslims. I like Muslims...with that being said, you are a Democrat. You are saying, 'Let's cut and run.' And I have to tell you, I have been nervous about this interview with you, because what I feel like saying is, 'Sir, prove to me that you are not working with our enemies.'" Ellison laughed it off and told the audience that he loved America, and Beck later apologized for the question's phrasing, but the host had basically implied the congressman was supporting terrorism. (Beck has since said in interviews that this is the moment in his career he regrets the most.)

*Come up and see me sometime...*Early in 2007, Beck had *US Weekly* editor Dina Sansing on to discuss racy photos that had emerged of an *American Idol* contestant, and he argued that women now had to be careful because photographers could be anywhere. When Sansing demurred, Beck said, out of the corner of his mouth, "Dina, I've got some time and a camera. Why don't you stop by?" Sansing ventured a tense smile, to which Beck responded, "No? OK."

Incidents such as these have collectively created a show that is, as *Rolling Stone* writer Matt Taibbi phrased it, "one of the weirdest news programs in American history," with a host who's "part comic, part carnival barker" and who, like many of his brethren, insists on calling his show entertainment and not news. While his popularity has soared among the younger set, Beck's cable ratings have slipped of late. In his first year he increased his CNN time slot's total viewer rating by 65 percent and his 25- to 54-year-old viewer rating by 85 percent, but after the 2006 midterm elections, the numbers dropped significantly. Nevertheless, Beck is still a key figure in the new infotainment landscape. With his face and voice attached to so many media outlets, it's worth examining how his reach came about.

Beck broke into radio at the age of 13, when he won a contest in Seattle to be a DJ for an hour. He went from there to hosting Christian radio, rock, and country programs when he wasn't in school; according to Beck, he was fired from them all on the same day for missing shifts. Then his mother killed herself. (Beck's brother also committed suicide, and another brother died of a heart attack.) "When my mother died, I just turned *dark*," Beck says.

After high school he worked for six months at a station in Provo, Utah, and then bounced around doing Top 40 at stations in Baltimore, Washington, Houston, and Phoenix, finally settling into the morning drive show at a station in Connecticut. He blames his family tragedies for his substance abuse, which led to a divorce from his first wife. The turning point came in a conversation with his father. "I only had two roads, kill myself or redeem myself," Beck has said.

Beck joined Alcoholics Anonymous and, with a letter of rec-
ommendation from Connecticut senator Joseph Lieberman, stud-
ied theology at Yale for a semester. He left the Roman Catholic
Church for the Church of Latter Day Saints, in which he is currently a proud missionary, along with his second wife and their
two adopted children. "I think God stalked me for a while," Beck
has said. "He threw Mormons in my path."

In 2000, Beck launched into talk radio at a Tampa, Florida, station, WFLA, and within a year the new *Glenn Beck Program* rock-
eted from 18th place to first. He fused humor and current events
in the Limbaugh mode, and after less than 18 months, Premiere
Radio Networks (a division of industry giant Clear Channel)
made him an offer to go national. He moved his home base to
Philadelphia, and when CNN offered him a deal four years later,
moved ship again to Radio City Music Hall in New York. He's still
there, offering a program that "is not about right and left, it's about
right and wrong" and describing himself as "not a Republican, nor
a Democrat. I'm a commonsense-thinking conservative."

But it's hard to find much common sense—or thinking—in
a statement like the one about Democratic presidential hopeful
Dennis Kucinich: "Every night I get down on my knees and pray
that Dennis Kucinich will burst into flames." Or the one about
filmmaker Michael Moore, in which he said, "I'm thinking about
killing Michael Moore, and I'm wondering if I could kill him myself, or if I would need to hire somebody to do it. No, I think I
could. I think he could be looking me in the eye, you know, and I
could just be choking the life out. Is this wrong?"

Beck also called former President Jimmy Carter "a waste of
skin" and said that, although North Korean dictator Kim Jong Il

was a bigger waste of skin, at least "his skin's being utilized by evil...
Who's utilizing the skin of Jimmy Carter?"

Beck loves to target liberals. He has said that Kucinich's wife
would have to be under the influence of "a date rape drug" to be
interested in her husband. He called *View* cohost Rosie O'Donnell
"a fat witch" with "blubber...just pouring out of her eyes." He has
retailed, along with Limbaugh, Hannity, and Savage, the discredited story that Barack Obama was trained in a madrassa. And he
has even stronger words about another Democratic presidential
candidate: "Hillary Clinton cannot be elected president because...
there's something about her vocal range...She is like the stereotypical—excuse the expression, but this is the way to—she's the
stereotypical bitch, you know what I mean?" Beck later qualified
his statement with, "I never said that Hillary Clinton was a bitch. I
said she sounded like one." Big distinction.

Beck has called Iraq war protester Cindy Sheehan "a tragedy
slut" and "a pretty big prostitute," and the father of murdered
American businessman Nicholas Berg "a scumbag" for speaking
out against President Bush's foreign policies. According to Beck,
Hurricane Katrina victims are also "scumbags" for rushing to get
the ATM relief cards that were handed out at the Astrodome. In the
same broadcast in which he made the Katrina remark, Beck said,
"It took me about a year to start hating the 9/11 victims' families...
I'm so sick of them because they're always complaining."

But the greatest recipients by far of Beck's vitriol have been
Muslims. In early 2007 he issued a strong warning to "All you
Muslims who have sat on your frickin' hands the whole time and
have not been marching in the streets and have not been saying,
'Hey, you know what? There are good Muslims and bad Muslims.

We need to be the first ones in the recruitment office lining up to shoot the bad Muslims in the head.'" He threatened that, if they didn't act quickly, they would be put in internment camps like Japanese Americans during World War II.

Beck has told his listeners that "the world is on the brink of World War III" and that the elements are in place for a global disaster he calls "the perfect storm." In November 2006, he hosted a television special called "Exposed: The Extremist Agenda," which contained clips of extremist Islamic rallies and anti-American cartoons. He is in favor of increasing America's military presence in Iraq and has also come down hard against other foreigners, strongly opposing the recent immigration legislation.

Beck sees the environmental movement as an insidious liberal plot to gain a foothold with the American public. He declared war on the animated movie *Happy Feet* for promoting an extremist environmentalist agenda. He has compared Al Gore with Adolf Hitler, saying both men used the same propaganda tactics:

"Al Gore's not going to be rounding up Jews and exterminating them. It is the same tactic, however. The goal is different. The goal is globalization. The goal is global carbon tax. The goal is the United Nations running the world. That is the goal. Back in the 1930s, the goal was get rid of all of the Jews and have one global government. You got to have an enemy to fight. And when you have an enemy to fight, then you can unite the entire world behind you, and you seize power. That was Hitler's plan. His enemy: the Jew. Al Gore's enemy, the U.N.'s enemy: global warming."

The Anti-Defamation League's subsequent denouncement of Beck's comments did not prevent the host from airing an hour-long special called "Exposed: The Climate of Fear" that contained falsehoods about the Earth's polar icecap and carbon dioxide levels as well as yet more Nazi comparisons. Beck has taken the title of Al Gore's film, *An Inconvenient Truth*, personally; his most recent outing was called "An Inconvenient Tour," and the title of his new best-selling book is *An Inconvenient Book*.

In his previous book, *The Real America: Messages from the Heart and Heartland*, Beck says that political correctness is "the classic Great Idea Gone Wrong. All it's done is shut us up...It's taken every opinion we have, it's taken every joke we have, and it's forced us to conceal it and hide it and bury it. It's made us superficial." In a sense these words could serve as the key to Beck's discourse: He offends us so that we may be offended and gives us strong words to try to make us think for ourselves. And our thinking should follow certain lines, as evidenced by another Beck quote, directed to a caller on his radio show: "Good for you, you have a heart, you can be a liberal. Now couple your heart with your brain and you can be a conservative."

Why is Glenn Beck so popular? Few things are as entertaining as listening to someone make outrageous remarks. The Beck spectacle is increased by the fact that the self-described "blowhard" might genuinely *be* deranged; Beck is like Hannity in that he truly seems to believe every word that comes out of his mouth. Like Savage, he'll attack anyone, regardless of party affiliation, and like Limbaugh, he'll often be quite funny doing it. He once said, "Sometimes I think that the biggest problem with G.W. [Bush] is that he just might be the worst communicating president since

Buchanan." He's not above making jokes at his own expense: "I don't have talent on loan from God," he says, "I have talent on loan from...maybe Lindsay Lohan."

Another aspect of Beck's popularity just may be the era we live in. The days of the staunch, respectful journalistic vanguard—think Edward R. Murrow and Walter Cronkite—are past; as a *New York Times* piece pointed out, the success of figures like Beck and fellow CNN cable train wreck Nancy Grace is part of a pronounced cultural shift from news-driven programming to personality- and opinion-driven programming with a newsy component. Journalists have given way to news personalities and in many respects, the stronger the personality, the more successfully the program registers. Above all, Glenn Beck is an original; there's no mistaking him for anyone else.

One can easily mistake him, however, for something that he isn't; the *Times* article quotes him as saying, "A younger audience is consuming news in a different way"—and the problem is his casual use of the word *news*. Although Beck of course says that he's not a journalist, his marketing, subject matter, and network placement lead audiences to regard him as one. The same obviously holds true for Limbaugh, Hannity, O'Reilly, and every other conservative talk show host who vows to bring his or her listeners the "truth."

One of Beck's big recent talking points, both on radio and on television, has been the possible reinstatement of the Fairness Doctrine. He has commiserated with everyone from CNN host Lou Dobbs to Michael Harrison over how his livelihood is being threatened along with his right to free speech. Shortly after he was named as a contributor to ABC's *Good Morning America* he said,

"Helping make sense of an increasingly complicated world is what I love to do." But for carnival barker Beck, making sense of a complicated world frequently becomes a simplistic affair.

6. NEAL BOORTZ:
Absolutely Anything Goes

Neal Boortz calls himself a libertarian. And while some of his views—nonviolent drug offenders should be released from prison; governmental interference in private lives should be minimized— emphasize the "liberty" in libertarian, most of his other opinions are as stone-cold conservative and downright offensive as those of rival hosts Beck and Savage. He's quick to call himself an entertainer (nicknaming Limbaugh "the Godfather" indicates how he'd like to model his image), but he's also the only talk radio host with a Wikipedia page dedicated exclusively to his controversies. His list of offenses chronicled by the watchdog site Media Matters puts even Imus to shame. The less-than-likable O'Reilly calls Boortz "a vicious son of a bitch."

Unlike other hosts, whose on-air personalities mix with their off-air ones, Boortz keeps his private life in the background, focusing less on himself than on the gravity of the "lessons" he wants to impart. He likes audiences to think he keeps lofty company; visitors to his Web site will find quotations from Voltaire, Dostoevsky, and Ayn Rand.

Born in Bryn Mawr, Pennsylvania, in 1945, the Army-brat son of a World War II fighter pilot soon moved with his family to Texas. He split his high school years—where he was by his own account a C-minus student—between California and Florida. Boortz first developed a passion for talk radio during his years as a student at Texas A&M, where he worked at the local broadcasting station under the pseudonym Randy Neal. He often had to work additional odd jobs to help support his family, including stints as a department store assistant and a carpenter. After a move to Atlanta, he became a fan of local radio host Herb Elfman; when Elfman committed suicide, Boortz showed up at the door of WRNG-AM to offer himself as a replacement. Surprisingly, he got the job.

He still lives in and broadcasts out of Atlanta, where his standard-format show—monologues, interviews, banter with producers, and important caller time—is syndicated by Cox Radio Network. Notwithstanding a degree from John Marshall Law School (he had his own practice for 16 years), Boortz now considers broadcasting daily to 4 million listeners his full-time job.

Like many other conservative talk radio hosts, Boortz pushed hard to kill the immigration bill. He once said you could identify the Latinos at a PTA meeting by their sombreros and their bandoliers. He also suggested that profit be made by selling tacos to Mexicans ramming themselves against a dividing border fence. Boortz said, "When we defeat this illegal alien amnesty bill and when we yank out the welcome mat, and they all start going back to Mexico, as a going away gift let's all give them a box of nuclear waste... and let 'em take it on down there to Mexico. Tell 'em it can—it'll heat tortillas." Needless to say, Boortz was ecstatic when the bipartisan, Bush-backed bill was defeated, but his history of racist remarks dates further back than the bill. More than a year earlier, he had suggested that the U.S. government use the Superdome in Louisiana to "store 11 million Hispanics just waiting to ship 'em back to Nicaragua, Colombia, Costa Rica, Mexico."

But his xenophobic ire is even more focused on Muslim Americans. Like Glenn Beck, Boortz believes that anything goes when it comes to protecting his country from outsiders, even if it means slandering an entire religion in the process. In one particularly vehement episode of his radio show, Boortz called Islam a "violent, violent religion" and said, "This Muhammad guy is just a phony rag picker" (a comment he later denied making during an appearance on *Larry King Live*). He added, "It is perfectly legitimate, perhaps even praiseworthy, to recognize Islam as a religion of vicious, violent, bloodthirsty cretins." At different times, he has also called all Muslims suicide bombers at heart, referred to Islam as "a deadly virus" and "a creeping mold infestation," and compared Muslims to cockroaches.

Boortz is quick to attack anyone he sees as sympathizing with Muslim interests. Former Democratic Representative Cynthia McKinney, a critic of both the Bush administration's post-9/11 penchant for secrecy and its handling of the Iraq war, has earned the label of "the cutest little Islamic jihadist in Congress." Boortz has called her a "ghetto slut," "ghetto trash," and "welfare drag queen." He apologized less than a week after making the last three remarks, but within three months he was back to his old ways, saying, "As sure as I'm going to stick my foot in my mouth...Cynthia McKinney will show her ass again." In a showing of his true colors, Boortz also said before the 2004 election that anyone who would vote for John Kerry was as big a threat to America as Osama bin Laden and his followers.

But one doesn't have to be Hispanic or Muslim to incur Boortz's wrath. One simply has to fall into one of his two main categories of scorn: the weak and the thuggish. To the first category belong the students at Columbine High School, who shouldn't have been counseled in the wake of the massacre at their school, and the victims of the Virginia Tech shootings, who in a show of pure cowardice let themselves be executed due to the "surrender-comply-adjust...doctrine of the left." Boortz has also criticized the "deadbeat" victims of Hurricane Katrina, calling them "complete bums, just debris" and suggesting that a female Katrina victim should resort to prostitution to support herself because "it sure beats the hell out of sucking off the taxpayers."

Boortz, who believes in a free-market economy with minimal government involvement, considers minimum-wage earners perhaps the "weakest" of all: "I want you to think for a moment of how incompetent and stupid and worthless, how—that's right, I used those words—how incompetent, how ignorant, how worthless is an adult that can't earn more than the minimum wage? You have to really, really, really be a pretty pathetic human being to not be able to earn more than the minimum wage." And in a staggering display of bluster, Boortz says if the United States were ever faced with impending disaster, the rich should be saved first.

Boortz, like many of his ilk, often identifies his adversaries by race. He predicted riots in California following ex-gang leader Stanley "Tookie" Williams's execution on the grounds that "there are a lot of aspiring rappers and NBA superstars who could really use a nice flat-screen television right now." He's also more than willing to classify thugs politically, as the title of his book *The Terrible Truth About Liberals* attests. In a 2003 WorldNetDaily.com article entitled "Democrats Abandon America," Boortz called "the congressional gargoyle" Dennis Kucinich and other Democrats irresponsible monsters for wanting to leave Iraq. He said that Hillary Clinton, neither as charming nor as attractive as Bill, is a menace because she wants to bring back the Fairness Doctrine.

There are some lines that Boortz will not cross; in the aftermath of Opie & Anthony's "Homeless Charlie" skit about the imagined violent sexual assault of Secretary of State Condoleezza Rice, First Lady Laura Bush, and the Queen of England, Boortz wrote a TownHall.com article arguing that the two hosts should be fired and removed from the airwaves "before their virus spreads." Boortz felt that Opie & Anthony gave political talk radio a bad name and made radio talkers like Sean Hannity and Boortz himself into targets for "power-hungry politicians." He argued that a "Hush Rush" bill purportedly aimed at bringing back the long-defunct Fairness Doctrine could effectively silence him, too.

But it's become increasingly difficult to silence Boortz—aka the High Priest, the Talkmaster, and Mighty Whitey, some of his self-bestowed nicknames. In addition to his radio show, Boortz publishes a blog called Nealz Nuze on his Web site and writes regularly for WorldNetDaily. He's the author of four books: three contain his regular talking points and the fourth, *The FairTax Book* (coauthored with Georgia congressman John Linder), puts forth a proposal to replace the IRS and all regular taxes with a single national retail sales tax. Boortz insists that he donates all profits from sales of the book to charity and that he has not made a penny from sales.

With his hatemongering sentiments passed off as entertainment, Neal Boortz is now high on anyone's list of political shock jocks. He may not rank in the top five among nationally syndicated talk radio hosts in popularity, but he's certainly near the top in toxicity.

7. LAURA INGRAHAM
The Razor Behind the Laughter

Laura Ingraham is...different. Not only is Ingraham younger than many other conservative radio personalities (at 45, she's more than a decade from Limbaugh's cohort), and the only female among them, but she also brings to the airwaves a snarky brand of aggressive humor fused with an attack-dog sensibility that she expresses with a chalk-on-gravel voice. Her goal is not to assert her own glory, but to rip apart her enemies, which include everyone from liberals and "elites" to, from time to time, even President Bush and presidential hopeful John McCain. Her style of argumentation is barebones simple; in a 1997 piece for Salon.com, Eric Alterman wrote that Ingraham *just laughed* in response to a position he took on television during the 1996 election. How could he counter that?

Ingraham often uses laughter as a weapon. One of her show's most popular parodies, "But...Monkey," interposes the sound of a screeching monkey over a sound bite from a political figure. Victims have included Democratic senators Harry Reid and Barbara Boxer as well as conservative figures like columnist Charles Krauthammer. Other regular segments include "Deep Thought of the Day" and "Lie of the Day." Ingraham also makes great use of pop culture clips (she plays the theme song from the television show *Flipper* when discussing John Kerry), and her production values are generally superb. Like many other successful hosts, she is often very funny, and her rapid-fire pacing and easy banter with her younger male producers (all three are in their early 20s) has more in common with the liberal *Stephanie Miller Show* than the hard-line commentary sometimes heard on conservative talk shows. At a deeper level, however, despite the comedy, Ingraham takes what she does quite seriously.

The rabid nature of her assault against immigration reform is a good example. Ingraham has perhaps been more strongly anti-immigration than any other talk personality except Michael Savage. Her show even features a regular segment called "The Illegal Immigration Sob Story" alert, in which she reads news pieces she feels are biased towards illegal immigrants. When she had White House spokesman Tony Snow on her program, she began by asking him why the Bush administration was dragging its heels on immigration reform. After sarcastically apologizing for interrupting his talking points, she said, "69 percent of Americans, 85 percent of the GOP, 55 percent of the Democrats want the border enforced. Does that affect you guys, or do you guys just blow it off?"

In the two-for-one combination that all too often serves conservative radio well, Ingraham once claimed that the immigration bill was an attempt by the mainstream media to make more people liberals. Anyone who still wonders whether talk radio had an influence on the bill's defeat should look at Ingraham's numbers; with more than 5 million weekly listeners, she is tied with Glenn Beck as the fourth most listened-to radio talk show host in America.

Alterman wrote that Ingraham's popularity is due to her having "something more important than knowledge or experience... She has star quality." She is also fearless; she once confronted CNN host John Roberts for calling her "outspoken," saying, "Do you guys introduce liberal commentators that way?" She's more aggressive than Limbaugh, more blatant than Hannity, and more rational than Beck or Savage, and although she often supports many of them (erroneously stating, for example, that Limbaugh never claimed the Clintons murdered Vince Foster), she is equally willing to call them out. She walked out of a *Hannity & Colmes* installment after the Don Imus "nappy-headed ho's" controversy was twisted into a discussion of Democratic vices, and once asked on her radio program after an appearance on *The O'Reilly Factor*, "Why is Bill O'Reilly afraid of George Soros?" (In the same broadcast Ingraham accused columnist Helen Thomas of working for Hezbollah, which has been identified by the U.S. government as a terrorist group.)

Ingraham was born and raised among the wealthy in Glastonbury, Connecticut, one of the state's richest suburbs, although her mother worked as a maid to support the family. She went to Dartmouth University and became the first female editor of the conservative *Dartmouth Review*, where conservative author Dinesh D'Souza, a former boyfriend, also worked. While there, she secretly sent a reporter with a tape recorder to a campus Gay Students Association meeting; she then outed the students in print and sent tapes of the meetings to the students' parents. In the magazine she called association members "cheerleaders for latent campus sodomites." (In 1997, more than a decade later, she wrote an article in the *Washington Post* detailing how she had changed her views in light of her brother Curtis's coming out as gay.)

After graduating from Dartmouth, she went to work for the White House as a speechwriter; like her peers, conservative radio talkers Mark Levin and Hugh Hewitt, Ingraham began her professional career as a Reagan employee. She also obtained a law degree from the University of Virginia and clerked for Justice Clarence Thomas. In 1995 she appeared on the cover of the *New York Times*

Magazine—wearing a friend's hip, leopard-print miniskirt—to illustrate an article about rising young conservatives. She then became both a regular MSNBC pundit and a commentator on the CBS Evening News, where she once asked Israeli prime minister Shimon Peres if the United States should bomb Libya or Syria in retaliation for a TWA flight explosion whose cause was unknown.

Ingraham argues politics the way lawyers argue cases, as if there can be no possible interpretation other than her own. She is a class-A schmoozer who understands and exploits her verbal gifts to the fullest. Her skill for networking, along with her willingness to go for the jugular, has allowed her to break into the boys' club of conservative radio.

In the late 1990s, she briefly hosted her own MSNBC cable television show *Watch It!* (17 months and three time slots later, she joked that it should have been called *Watch It Get Canceled!*), and then, in 2001, launched *The Laura Ingraham Show* on radio. Ingraham's particular blend of humor and argument apparently translated more effectively on radio than on television, and the Talk Radio Network now syndicates her show on nearly 325 terrestrial stations (it's also available on Sirius and XM satellite radio). She has survived both a breast cancer scare and a broken wedding engagement, and continues to mock the establishment sardonically for three hours daily.

Ingraham has made more than her share of controversial comments, with frequent guest appearances on television affording her as much prominence as her radio work (for someone whose own television show was relatively short-lived, she spends a tremendous amount of time on other people's programs). She's no Neal Boortz, but she's certainly more outrageous than, say, Hugh

Hewitt. In one of her most famous incidents, on Election Day 2006 Ingraham encouraged listeners to jam the phone line of a toll-free Democratic Party service for reporting voting problems. No tangible consequences came of it (the Democrats won anyway), but it did put Democratic senator Patrick Leahy up in arms.

Perhaps the greatest controversy of Ingraham's career, however, came from comments she made about the Iraq war. In March of 2006, Ingraham went on a six-day tour of Iraq, visiting hospitals, orphanages, and Iraqi villages. Upon returning to the United States, she appeared on NBC's *Today Show* to criticize the mainstream American media for its unwillingness to report "the truth" of the Iraq situation. She said that NBC had focused on programming "Where in the World is Matt Lauer?" and that "to do a show from Iraq means to talk to the Iraqi military, to go out with the Iraqi military, to actually have a conversation with the people instead of reporting from hotel balconies about the latest IEDs going off."

Washington Post writer Jonathan Finer later reported that Ingraham "rarely, if ever, spent a moment outside the protection of U.S. forces or a night outside a military base." Finer compared her experience with that of the Iraq-stationed journalists she criticized, "almost all of whom operate without military protection." While the *National Review*'s Tim Graham applauded Ingraham for bringing out the "facts the media self-defense teams ignore," MSNBC host Keith Olbermann said on his show *Countdown* that Ingraham had dishonored the memory of the 80 American journalists killed and others kidnapped in Iraq, and that her comment "was not only unforgivable of her, it was desperate and it was stupid."

Ingraham's stance on women's issues is divided at best; around the time of Clarence Thomas's Supreme Court appointment, she joined with a conservative group called Independent Women's Forum that formed a committee to attack and discredit Anita Hill's sexual harassment testimony against Thomas. (Independent Women's Forum's other activities included testifying in Congress for defunding the Violence Against Women Act and against affirmative action.) While she has criticized Fox for gratuitous, sexually explicit programming and helped lead a media campaign against the misogynistic rapper Akon, she also cohosted a three-part PBS special on "the gender wars," which explored "whether the advancement of women in virtually all areas of society can be achieved without a retreat, in some way, on the part of men." One need not guess where Ingraham, a convert to Roman Catholicism, stands on a woman's right to choose.

Among prominent female political figures, Hillary Clinton in particular provokes Ingraham's ire. Her first book, *The Hillary Trap*, tried hard to make the case that Clinton was actually setting women's rights back by arguing for special status for them. "The complaints of Western feminists look like petty self-absorption when you line them up against human rights abuses in Third World military dictatorships," Ingraham wrote.

Ingraham also argues that a vocal minority—the "elites"—are threatening American values, and they should pipe down for the majority's sake. Elites include antiwar demonstrators and university professors ("It's well known that in the 1960s, leftists conquered the academies"). There is also no love lost between Ingraham and Europeans, who she believes fail to understand and appreciate America's love for "God, guns, and the death penalty."

Ingraham's third book, *Power to the People*, was released on September 11, 2007. The patriotic timing was deliberate; the book is partly memoir but is mostly devoted to annihilating what she calls the "pornification" of America, an increasing cultural tendency towards flaunted sexuality and the loss of traditional values. She calls the book "a rallying cry for common sense and good old-fashioned American ideals of patriotism, family, faith, and country," one that encourages people to take matters into their own hands. In its first week, the book ranked third on the Amazon bestseller list.

"We are the government," Ingraham said, in an interview promoting the book. Controlling people by telling them how to think for themselves is a nice piece of demagogic trickery, though hardly original among the conservative bloc that crowds talk radio today. Ingraham has proved to be a master at such trickery—and like her or not, she's every bit as funny, as appealing, and as dangerous as each of her male peers and friends.

8. MARK LEVIN
Attack of the Clones

"Are you a lib, sir?" The question comes from the irritating, irritable, high-pitched voice of the bearded, bald, New York–based talk radio host Mark Levin, and it's one of Levin's favorite questions to his callers. The word "lib" is practically an expletive to Levin, and the 50-year-old native Philadelphian is not ashamed to admit it. Rush Limbaugh calls him "F. Lee Levin," Sean Hannity calls him "The Great One," and in a great number of markets Levin's show follows theirs. He rules his time slot in New York, Dallas, Chicago, Detroit, and Washington, D.C., and he's on more than 130 stations with a weekly audience of more than 4 million listeners. He's a rising force on the conservative talk radio scene—the career he's always dreamed of.

As a 12-year-old growing up in Pennsylvania, Levin would fall asleep listening to the radio. At 16 he badgered WCAU in Philadelphia into letting him host a show one day for an hour. He skipped his senior year of high school, finished college in three years, and graduated from Temple Law School when he was only 22. He took a job the following year in the Reagan administration and served in several positions throughout the Cabinet, rising as high as chief of staff to Attorney General Edwin Meese. He founded his own public interest law firm, the Landmark Legal Foundation in Virginia, and in 1995 became an unofficial legal and constitutional consultant to Limbaugh, who at the time was not only the most successful talk radio host in America but popular enough in conservative circles to have influenced the previous year's congressional elections.

Levin also became a frequent guest commentator on Hannity's show, occasionally filling in for the host when he was sick or on vacation. In 2002 WABC's program director, Phil Boyce, approached Levin with an offer to host a Sunday afternoon show without pay; Levin accepted, and 14 months later he was promoted to a paying job on weeknights. He became ensconced within the 6:00–8:00 p.m. time slot and rapidly grew popular enough to earn a syndication deal from ABC in February 2007.

Levin is entertaining; he's bright, sarcastic, and often enraged, with an unforgettable nasal roar, but he's just as popular for the endorsements he holds and the company he keeps. In 2001 the American Conservative Union gave Levin its Ronald Reagan Award for distinguished fidelity to the conservative cause. Unlike his Foxified peers, Sean Hannity and Bill O'Reilly, Levin makes no pretense of objectivity; in fact, he has stated forthrightly, "I'm unfair and unbalanced."

A recent President Bush nominee for the U.S. 4th Circuit Court of Appeals, Steve A. Matthews, is on the Landmark Legal Foundation board of directors. Two of Landmark's most recent projects have been investigating the Environmental Protection Agency and other environmental organizations "for both the amount and misuse of federal grants by these organizations," and nominating Rush Limbaugh for the Nobel Peace Prize.

This points to another set of endorsements and influences Levin has, not just from the general conservative party but specifically from industry leaders Limbaugh and Hannity. He follows them in many ways—literally, in that his time slot comes after theirs, but also in the formation of his identity as a radio talk show host. Hannity and Levin frequently call in to one another's shows and refer to each other as "Doctor." Levin's show has been obviously influenced by many of Hannity's on-air tactics, including patriotic demonstrations; when a Marine father calls the show, Levin will play the Marine hymn before paying homage to all of America's armed forces. He also shares many opinions with his mentors, including their dismissal of global warming as a hoax and their insistence that conservative talk radio is an antidote to the "liberal media," taking the position that Hillary Clinton and other ne'er-do-wells wish to destroy conservative talk through the reimposition of the Fairness Doctrine.

In the aftermath of the *Washington Post*'s reporting on former Virginia senator George Allen's use of the word "macaca," Levin said that the *Post* was trying "to smear George Allen...These are tactics that you see in totalitarian regimes, where false information is put out there so often that a frenzy almost builds up around it... But one good thing we have now that we didn't have back then is talk radio." For Levin, conservative talk radio is a safe haven from the liberal media's otherwise ubiquitous and oppressive regime.

Levin also shares his mentors' love of using erroneous analogies to prove a point, as when he compared John Kerry to Benedict Arnold. Levin even apes specific comments; two days after Limbaugh referred to the U.N. General Assembly as "thugs and dictators," Levin compared the United Nations to the Ku Klux Klan and said, "They've got people...that are torturers, mass murderers, anti-Semites, anti-Americans, antifreedom..."

Despite his growing stable of radio affiliates, Levin still has yet to amass anywhere near the attention that Limbaugh or Hannity has received. He has been a regular talk host for only five years, and his angry intelligence lacks the memorable sound bites delivered by Hannity or Limbaugh. The two most popular talk hosts in America are successful with entirely different styles; Levin may play the patriot card or make jokes about Nancy "Stretch" Pelosi, as he did on a *Hannity* installment, but he has yet to refine his technique. Mostly, Levin is just a smaller version of his twin heroes.

Levin is best known, in fact, not for his work in radio but in print; his 2005 book *Men in Black: How the Supreme Court Is Destroying America*, with a forward by Limbaugh, arrived at number three on the *New York Times* bestseller list. The book argues that the Supreme Court is made up of "activist judges" who aim to seize power from the legislative and executive branches of the American government and use it themselves; each of the first three chapters ends with the word "tyranny."

The book, published by Regnery Publishing, the same group that put out *Unfit for Combat: The Swift Boat Veterans Speak Out Against John Kerry*, was not reviewed by either the *New York Times* or the *Washington Post*; in a *Post* piece written about its surprising popularity, Emory University law professor and Supreme Court historian David Garrow said, "The fascinating thing is that it's a bestseller on a subject where 100 percent of us who present ourselves as experts haven't read it." In her review of the book for Slate.com, Dahlia Lithwick wrote, "The reason it may take you only slightly longer to read *Men in Black* than it took Levin to write it is that you'll experience an overwhelming urge to shower between chapters."

Nonetheless, Levin's popularity is steadily growing, buoyed by the active support that superstars like Limbaugh, Hannity, and their associates give him. Levin's current status proves a valuable point about conservative talk radio figures, formats, and commercial acceptance: the genre has historically been so successful that syndicators would rather program inexperienced, unprofessional figures who resemble current stars than seek out someone new and different. Being smart and funny is important in radio, but so is having the right friends in all the right places, as Mark Levin can easily attest.

9. HUGH HEWITT
Talk Radio's Karl Rove

Hugh Hewitt, a white-haired, slightly porcine native of Warren, Ohio, who has risen rapidly to the top of the conservative pundit food chain, is different from most other talkers. His broadcast audience is smaller (*The Hugh Hewitt Show* reaches 112 stations nationally, about a sixth of the number enjoyed by Limbaugh), and he's more subdued than other hosts. While cohorts like Beck and Savage make shocking remarks daily about women and minorities, the most openly offensive thing Hewitt might say is that the war in Iraq is proceeding according to plan. Unlike hosts who bully their guests and callers, Hewitt lets people talk and sounds genuinely interested in what they have to say. Like Hannity, Hewitt will often let others articulate his ideas for him; by having Laura Ingraham on his show to decry the immigration bill, Hewitt is able to impose his beliefs upon listeners without taking flack for espousing them directly. If Limbaugh is the President Bush of talk radio, with Hannity its Cheney and Savage its Rumsfeld, then Hugh Hewitt can easily pass as its Karl Rove.

Hewitt will promote his beliefs by whatever means necessary, using every medium at his disposal. More than any other conservative talker, Hewitt has given conservatives a presence on the Web. "It strikes me that blogging, more than radio, is Hewitt's central passion," wrote Nicholas Lemann in a *New Yorker* profile of the host. Hewitt has a slightly different view of how TownHall.com, his Internet home base, works in tandem with the radio show. "Both spoken words and written words are powerful," he says. "Acting in harmony, the effect is exponential." Hewitt keeps two computers next to his microphone, and during commercial breaks he uploads quotes to his blog or reads news articles. In remarking on the death of traditional journalistic practices, Hewitt has said:

"There is too much expertise, all of it almost instantly available now, for the traditional idea of journalism to last much longer. In the past, almost every bit of information was difficult and expensive to acquire and was therefore mediated by journalists whom readers and viewers were usually in no position to second-guess. Authority has drained from journalism for a reason. Too many of its practitioners have been easily exposed as poseurs."

The solution is twofold: first, to gather information from as many different sources as possible; and second, to work the hardest at presenting it and consequently be the best. Hewitt has successfully stirred some online activism; after posting a link to Senator Rick Santorum's campaign funding database, donations increased by 500 percent. "It's not about getting people angry," Hewitt remarked. "It's about being effective."

Although Hewitt does occasionally make controversial remarks (as a guest on Chris Matthews's television program he put forth distortions about President Bush's proposed plan to change the Social Security system), he is more focused on spotlighting what he sees as biases and flaws in the mainstream media or, as he calls it, "the MSM." Hewitt labels his show "National Public Radio for Conservatives." He frequently grills guest journalists on their political beliefs, questioning their views on the military and asking which candidate they voted for in the last presidential election.

As for the host's own beliefs, he is proudly and transparently of the Republican faith, expressing admiration for many of the Grand Old Party's leading figures. President George W. Bush is the victim of unfair media criticism; Republican senator Jon Kyl of Arizona, architect of the recently destroyed immigration bill, is beleaguered and underappreciated; and Rush Limbaugh is "the most trusted journalist in America." Hewitt has also been unafraid of touting his Christianity; *Atlantic* writer Andrew Sullivan identified him as someone who believes that "religion dictates politics and that politics should dictate the laws for everyone, Christian and non-Christian alike."

While Hewitt has stayed blind to certain negative aspects of the religious right, he's too bright and sophisticated to be an ordinary Bible-thumper. This bespectacled busy man of the airwaves graduated *cum laude* with an A.B. in government from Harvard in the late 1970s, then was a ghostwriter for Richard Nixon for five years before enrolling at law school at the University of Michigan. He held several different posts within the Reagan administration, including special assistant for Attorney General Edwin Meese and deputy director of the U.S. Office of Personnel Management. After Reagan he went back to Nixon, overseeing the construction of the Richard Nixon Library.

Hewitt then opened a law firm, at which he still practices (he also teaches constitutional law at Chapman University), and began to host a weekend talk radio show as well as a news program on a PBS affiliate in Los Angeles, for which he won three local Emmys. His hard-pressing, accessibly intellectual style grew until he was picked up by Salem Radio Networks, which gave him a radio show to add to his columnist, blogger, and editor positions at TownHall.com. His prolific writings mark another way in which Hewitt differs from his talk radio contemporaries; while other hosts view writing as a side gig, with a few books to tie in to their radio personalities and propagate their personal mythologies, Hewitt rightly sees himself as a legitimate author. Since 1996, he has churned out nine books, all generally no longer than 250 pages and most treating the themes dearest to Hewitt's heart: religion, new media, and dominating progressives. His most recent book, *A Mormon in the White House? 10 Things Every American Should Know About Mitt Romney*, is essentially a biography of Hewitt's favorite Republican presidential candidate, which argues that Americans should overcome their fear of Mormonism and vote for the best man for the job.

The question of who would or wouldn't vote for Romney underlines one of Hewitt's weaknesses: his tendency, like other conservative talkers, to embellish the facts. While Hewitt on several occasions claimed that voters on the left were the ones most leery of Romney's Mormonism, polls instead found that conservatives and evangelical Christians were in fact more hesitant to vote for a Mormon than liberals ever would be.

Hewitt often uses "the noisy left" as a convenient whipping boy, such as in discussions of the invasion and occupation of Iraq. His feelings for liberal opposition to the Bush administration's policies toward Iraq are perhaps best expressed in these words: "...a great deal of American mainstream media is invested in the idea that [the Iraq war] is a disaster...There's quite a lot not being covered, because to cover it, and to cover it extensively, will not only support the Bush administration decision to go to war here but make it appear as though one of the wisest he has made. And indeed, investment in the failure of this operation is what is bringing increased contempt for the American media across the land, except on the noisy left. And the noisy left doesn't win elections."

So Hewitt blogs and blathers on, neither the most attractive nor the most charismatic figure in the conservative landscape but nevertheless one of the brightest and most dedicated. When Nicholas Lemann wanted to profile Hewitt for the *New Yorker*, the host consented on one condition: that he be allowed to write his own piece on Lemann, who is dean of Columbia University's Graduate School of Journalism. (In his article, Hewitt critiqued Columbia's journalism program as hopelessly behind the times.) Lemann wrote that watching *The Hugh Hewitt Show* made him feel that "Hewitt's world is journalism's alternate universe." Lemann was only partly right. Rather than simply being an alternative to standard practices, Hugh Hewitt wants to create an entirely new form of journalism.

2008 TALKERS® 250

FEATURING THE

HEAVY HUNDRED™

THE 100 MOST IMPORTANT RADIO TALK SHOW HOSTS IN AMERICA

The editors of TALKERS magazine, with input from industry leaders, present the 250 Most Important Radio Talk Show Hosts in America — a popular annual feature that includes what has come to be known as the "Heavy Hundred." This is the second year that the Heavy Hundred are ranked in order of importance.

This is one of the most challenging tasks that TALKERS undertakes each year considering that there are some 5,000 talk show hosts across the country, ranging from national icons to those laboring in relative obscurity.

Aside from the hosts whose sheer numbers and fame demand their inclusion on this list, the selection process is subjective with the goal being to create a list reflective of the industry's diversity and total flavor as well as giving credit where credit is due.

The TALKERS magazine editors who painstakingly compile this super-list draw upon a combination of hard and soft factors when evaluating candidates. These include (in alphabetical order): courage, effort, impact, longevity, potential, ratings, recognition, revenue, service, talent and uniqueness. We acknowledge that it is as much art as science and that the results are arguable.

There is one concrete qualification for inclusion. Hosts must be working at the time TALKERS magazine goes to print with this issue in order to be considered. They must have a regularly scheduled professional show on the air at a minimum of one terrestrial station, satellite radio provider or Internet domain at press time.

TALKERS magazine salutes the fine broadcasters who made this year's list.

2008 TALKERS® HEAVY HUNDRED™

1 Rush Limbaugh
Premiere Radio Networks

Remains the most listened-to issues talk host. Twenty years in national syndication and the pioneer of modern-day political talk.

Tel. 212-445-3900 • www.rushlimbaugh.com

2 Sean Hannity
ABC Radio Networks

News/talk's multi-media superstar with more than 12.5 million weekly listeners.

Tel. 212-613-3800 • www.hannity.com

3 Michael Savage
Talk Radio Network

Talk radio's leading independent conservative. Unapologetic, non-partisan critic. Controversial and funny.

Tel. 541-664-8827 • www.michaelsavage.com

4 Dr. Laura Schlessinger
Take On The Day, LLC

The industry's most listened-to female host. Enormous ratings among women listeners.

Tel. 212-239-2988 • www.drlaura.com

5 Glenn Beck
Premiere Radio Networks

Major star in the talk radio business. Unique brand of humor permeates his multi-media endeavors.

Tel. 818-377-5300 • www.glennbeck.com

2008 TALKERS® HEAVY HUNDRED™

6 Laura Ingraham
Talk Radio Network

*The top female issues-talk host
with multi-media presence.
More than 5 million weekly listeners.*

Tel. 541-664-8827 • www.lauraingraham.com

7 Don Imus
ABC Radio Networks

*Controversial, colorful broadcasting
legend heard in New York and
national syndication. Makes waves and news.*

Tel. 212-613-3800 • www.wabcradio.com

8 Ed Schultz
Jones Radio Networks/P1

*Still the lead dog in the progressive talk pack.
Nationally syndicated and local show in Fargo.*

Tel. 701-237-5346 • www.bigeddieradio.com

9 Mike Gallagher
Salem Radio Network

*Thirty-year talk radio pro heard nationally
on more than 200 stations. Solid performer.*

Tel. 972-831-1920 • www.mikeonline.com

10 Neal Boortz
Jones Radio Networks

*Almost four decades in the talk radio
business. An original. Nationally syndicated
to some 150 affiliates.*

Tel. 404-897-7500 • www.boortz.com

2008 TALKERS® HEAVY HUNDRED™

11   Bill O'Reilly
Westwood One

A conservative icon in American talk media. Heard on more than 400 stations.

Tel. 212-641-2000 • www.billoreilly.com

12   Dave Ramsey
The Dave Ramsey Show

The biggest brand in the life and financial advice genre.

Tel. 877-410-3283 • www.daveramsey.com

13   Howard Stern
Sirius Satellite Radio

The father of hot talk radio. The most listened-to satellite talk host.

Tel. 212-867-1200 • www.howardstern.com

14   Mancow
TRN-FM

High-energy, youthful approach to issues talk. Fast-growing FM morning drive presence. Big national profile.

Tel. 541-664-8827 • www.mancow.com

15   Mark Levin
ABC Radio Networks

Conservative talk host enjoying meteoric rise in ratings and affiliates.

Tel. 212-613-3800 • www.marklevinshow.com

2008 TALKERS® HEAVY HUNDRED™

16 Alan Colmes
Fox News Radio

*Late-night progressive talk host
with huge national profile.*

Tel. 212-301-3000 • www.alan.com

17 Opie & Anthony
CBS Radio/XM

*Leading practitioners of hot talk. Topical and
humorous. Heard on satellite and terrestrial radio.
Gregg "Opie" Hughes and Anthony Cumia.*

Tel. 310-459-3728 • www.opieandanthony.com

18 Joe Madison
WOL

*Nation's leading African-American
activist talk host. Major force in
Washington, DC with global impact.*

Tel. 301-429-2631 • www.joemadison.com

19 Bill Handel
KFI

*Gigantic numbers in morning drive in
Los Angeles. Also does syndicated
weekend law show.*

Tel. 818-559-2252 • www.kfi640.com

20 Michael Medved
Salem Radio Network

*Outstanding analyst of politics and
pop culture. More than 3.75
million weekly listeners.*

Tel. 206-621-1793 • www.michaelmedved.com

2008 TALKERS® HEAVY HUNDRED™

21 Doug Stephan
Stephan Productions

Prolific general issues/lifestyles personality hosting broad-appeal syndicated morning show plus weekend specialty programs.

Tel. 650-654-3969 • www.dougstephan.com

22 Jim Bohannon
Westwood One

Popular late-night generalist talk host. Seasoned pro with diverse audience.

Tel. 202-457-7978 • www.jimbotalk.net

23 Thom Hartmann
KPOJ/Air America Radio

Major star in the progressive talk genre. Intellectual approach to lib talk. Prolific author.

Tel. 503-323-6400 • www.thomhartmann.com

24 Jerry Doyle
Talk Radio Network

Renaissance man with independent conservative tack. Growing in national syndication.

Tel. 541-664-8827 • www.jerrydoyle.com

25 Bill Bennett
Salem Radio Network

Heard nationwide in morning drive. More than 3 million weekly listeners for this historic political figure.

Tel. 703-248-9413 • www.bennettmornings.com

2008 TALKERS® HEAVY HUNDRED™

26 George Noory
Premiere Radio Networks

*Late-night radio's king of paranormal talk.
More than 3 million weekly listeners.*

Tel. 818-377-5300 • www.coasttocoastam.com

27 Lars Larson
Westwood One/KXL

*Hard-working conservative talk host with
journalism pedigree. Does national
and local Portland shows daily.*

Tel. 503-243-7595 • www.larslarson.com

28 Stephanie Miller
Jones Radio Networks/WYD Media

*L.A.-based syndicated progressive talk host with
comic bent. Unique and respected star who
stretches beyond the lib-talk genre.*

Tel. 917-881-9669 • www.stephaniemiller.com

29 Jim Rome
Premiere Radio Networks

*Twelve years in national syndication as
one of sports talk's most listened-to hosts.
More than 200 affiliates.*

Tel. 818-377-5300 • www.jimrome.com

30 Clark Howard
Jones Radio Networks

*The talk industry's number one
consumer-issues host with more than
3.25 million weekly listeners.*

Tel. 404-897-7500 • www.clarkhoward.com

2008 TALKERS® HEAVY HUNDRED™

31

Lionel

Air America Radio

Witty, satirical, intellectual talk host heard in syndication mid-mornings.

Tel. 212-871-8100 • www.lionelonline.com

32

John & Ken

KFI

Afternoon drive ratings juggernaut in Los Angeles. Commandeer local issues. John Kobylt and Ken Chiampou.

Tel. 818-559-2252 • www.johnandkenshow.com

33

Tom Leykis

Westwood One

Consistent performer in hot talk genre. Solid audience on big FM signals.

Tel. 323-971-9710 • www.blowmeuptom.com

34

Jack Rice

WCCO

Unique brand of journalistic talk radio from this lawyer and former intelligence community official. A rising star headed for greatness.

Tel. 612-370-0611 • thejackriceshow.blogspot.com

35

Dennis Prager

Salem Radio Network

Growing audience and affiliate base for one of the business' top moralist and intellectual talk hosts. Loyal following.

Tel. 818-956-5552 • www.dennisprager.com

2008 TALKERS® HEAVY HUNDRED™

36 Kim Komando
WestStar TalkRadio Network

The talk radio industry's leading personality in computer talk. Over 2.25 million weekly listeners.

Tel. 602-381-8200 • www.komando.com

37 Dr. Joy Browne
WOR Radio Network

The preeminent talk radio relationship doc. Evenings in New York and in syndication.

Tel. 212-642-4529 • www.drjoy.com

38 Spike O'Dell
WGN

Earns huge numbers at legendary Chicago signal.

Tel. 312-222-4700 • www.wgnradio.com

39 Doug McIntyre
KABC

Morning drive issues talk in Los Angeles. Experienced and unique performer with showbiz background.

Tel. 310-840-4900 • www.kabc.com

40 Randi Rhodes
Air America Radio

Clever, insightful and brash purveyor of progressive issues talk radio.

Tel. 212-871-8100 • www.therandirhodesshow.com

CHAPTER 4

Fear of Fairness

Eliminate talk radio and America goes down the tubes.
—Joseph Farah, WorldNetDaily.com

In the summer of 2007, fresh on the heels of their success in defeating the immigration bill, right-wing radio talkers immediately
moved *en masse* to consideration of a new topic—fairness and
free speech, or the lack thereof. As reported in the industry trade
journal *Broadcasting & Cable*, "With a talk lineup that includes
Rush Limbaugh, Sean Hannity, and Mark Levin, WMAL(AM)
Washington was among the column of conservative talk-radio stations that helped last month to dash President Bush's dreams of
signing an immigration reform bill. Now the station is joining the
fight over an issue that speaks directly to its proud tagline: 'Free
speech heard here.'"

Was the threat to the First Amendment real, or was it invented
to drive up ratings and create outrage? The conservative talkers
focused on the fairly remote possibility that a hoary, defunct FCC
regulation known as the Fairness Doctrine, adopted in 1949 and
enforced only sporadically until President Ronald Reagan effec-

tively killed it in 1987, might return under some future Democratic administration and somehow wipe conservative talk radio from the media landscape.

Calling the Reagan-era demise of the doctrine "the decision that launched a thousand lips," *Los Angeles Times* reporter Jim Puzzanghera noted, "The move is widely credited with triggering the explosive growth of political talk radio." But when a handful of politicians mused about its reinstatement "after conservative talk show hosts such as Rush Limbaugh, Sean Hannity, and Michael Savage helped torpedo a major immigration bill," the result was an "armada of opposition on the airwaves, Internet blogs, and in Washington, where broadcasters have joined with Republicans to fight what they call an attempt to zip their lips."

Many liberals were predictably suspicious of the right's new-found crusade, and some, including radio talk show host Ed Schultz, characterized rumors of a reinstated Fairness Doctrine as a "straw man" invented by conservatives. "They have 450 right-wing talkers in America," Schultz said. "They all read off the same talking points."

As *Broadcasting & Cable* noted, the Fairness Doctrine had "long been the province of communications law texts and history books. But in recent weeks, conservative talkers have seized upon—and amplified—a burgeoning legislative debate over re-instating the doctrine, making it a hot topic on radio and major television news programs."

The original Fairness Doctrine required broadcasters—who must obtain a license to use the publicly owned airwaves—to present issues of public importance in a balanced manner. Since the doctrine was an attempt to ensure balanced coverage of controversial issues, and since it hadn't been enforced in two decades, the sudden and fervent talk show opposition to it seemed odd at first blush. After all, don't conservatives regularly claim an interest in being "fair and balanced"?

Nevertheless, merely the *perceived possibility* of bringing back the Fairness Doctrine made many conservative commentators apoplectic, leading some to paint that possibility in near-apocalyptic terms. Former House Speaker Newt Gingrich called it "an assault on the First Amendment" and accused Democrats of wanting to wipe out conservative talk radio. "They want to kill it because every time we have an extended conversation with the American people, liberalism falls apart and its ideas collapse," Gingrich explained. America's number one radio talker, Rush Limbaugh, even went so far as to suggest that, instead of a Fairness Doctrine, perhaps a "Truth Doctrine" should be imposed to control all news outlets other than talk radio.

Other conservative voices, such as Joseph Farah of WorldNetDaily.com, picked up on Limbaugh's lead and began warning readers explicitly of an impending "war on talk radio." In an article in the August 2007 special issue of WND's *Whistleblower* magazine, Farah wrote, "Though most Americans aren't yet aware of it, talk radio—from Rush Limbaugh to the local talker in small-town America—is under major attack." Farah drew a direct link between talk radio's success in mobilizing opinion against the immigration bill and what he and other conservatives saw as a frontal assault on their main medium of expression. "And no wonder: last month radio talkers presided over a minor American revolution when they urged millions of citizens to successfully oppose the immigration/amnesty bill that the president and both political parties had been pushing relentlessly," Farah wrote. "It went down in flames—a devastating blow to the political establishment.

"Now it's revenge time," he concluded, articulating the conventional conservative wisdom. "If radio talkers, in conjunction with the Internet, can mobilize Americans to oppose the political elite with regard to immigration, what kind of effect might they have on voters during the critically important November 2008 presidential election just around the corner? The fact is, powerful forces in and out of politics feel extremely threatened by this one part of the mass media that overwhelmingly champions traditional American values...They want talk radio crippled before it does any more 'damage.'"

Some other "highlights" of the *Whistleblower* issue included:

- "Al-Qaida and the Fairness Doctrine," by Joseph Farah.
- "The Real Fight Over Talk Radio Is Yet to Come," by James L. Gattuso, who shows that radio censors have many other weapons beyond the Fairness Doctrine.
- "Congress and the Un-Fairness Doctrine," which "reveals how historically both political parties have used the pretense of 'fairness' to ruthlessly thwart their opposition."
- "The Day 'New Media' Was Born," which reveals that the "forward thinking of none other than Ronald Reagan" facilitated the explosion of talk radio.
- "Claim: Hillary, Boxer Look to 'Fix' Talk Radio," in which Senator James Inhofe says his Democrat colleagues want to take legislative action.

- "The Imus Lynch Party," by Pat Buchanan, showing what's really behind the attacks by Sharpton and Jackson.
- "'It's Not Just Imus,' Warn Talk Radio Headhunters," a "chilling survey of attacks on top talkers" like Rush Limbaugh and Michael Savage for alleged "hate speech."
- "CAIR'S [Council on American-Islamic Relations] War on Talk Radio," by Michelle Malkin, which purportedly showed "how the controversial Islamic group is pushing for the Al Jazeera-fication of America's airwaves."
- "3 Sneak Attacks Coming Against Talk Radio," detailing the methods for regulating the airwaves "most favored by anti-talk-radio activists."
- "Air America Recovering After Bankruptcy Woes," profiling "how the left-leaning radio network is doing" since it filed for Chapter 11 protection.
- "Why Can't Liberal Talk Radio Succeed?" by Hal Lindsey, who "insightfully points out that although some leftist hosts may be funny, their opinions aren't convincing."

And finally:

- "God, Man and Talk radio," by veteran talker Bob Just, on the rise and fall of the "secular media monopoly."

In reality, the sudden conservative focus on the possible return of the Fairness Doctrine, as expressed on right-wing radio talk shows, seemed consciously designed to generate more heat than light and to be more devoted to stirring up the base and exciting the audience than combating any real danger. Most informed political observers believe there is scant possibility that the fusty doctrine will ever be reimposed—and even less chance that if it were, talk radio would be "eliminated."

Far from an assault on the Constitution or on "traditional American values," the doctrine was actually aimed at encouraging free speech by prohibiting individual stations or station groups from presenting just one point of view on major issues. No station or group of stations, for example, could broadcast exclusively right-wing hosts offering exclusively right-wing opinions (sound familiar?). After all, radio broadcasts are only possible through the use of billions of dollars' worth of public airwaves—airwaves that once came with a sense of responsibility and at least a tacit understanding that broadcasters were somehow part of a public trust.

Given the broadcasters' licensed use of publicly owned airwaves, the Fairness Doctrine—whatever its flaws—was initially deemed an appropriate governmental mechanism for ensuring balance and promoting democratic discussion. In its absence—decades after its imposition and 20 years after its effective suspension—news-and-opinion radio talk has clearly come to be dominated by avowed conservatives. Chief among them is Limbaugh, who says he doesn't really fear the return of the Fairness Doctrine. "When I started there were 125 talk stations. Today there are 2,000. The idea that there are fewer ideas expressed, that there is less diversity, is absurd," Limbaugh told *National Review* writer Byron York. He concluded, "I don't think this has a prayer."

Despite the unlikelihood of the Fairness Doctrine's return, other conservatives found even the suggestion so repugnant that Indiana's Republican representative Mike Pence—a talk radio host himself before he was elected to Congress—was led to introduce the "Broadcaster Freedom Act," which would deny the FCC the "resources or authority" to reinstate the doctrine.

"It is a dangerous proposal to suggest the government should be in the business of rationing free speech," Pence said on the House floor. "Congress must take action to ensure that the archaic remnant of a bygone era of American radio does not return. There is nothing fair about the Fairness Doctrine."

Three Republican senators—John Thune of South Dakota and Norm Coleman of Minnesota, along with Arizona's John McCain—took the lead in supporting Pence's effort. "Talk radio has flourished due to free market ideas," Coleman said, parroting the line taken by the right-wing radio talkers. "We live in...a world in which you can simply change the dial or turn the radio off. But we don't want government in the business of censoring or monitoring and applying a standard that is basically unfair." Jim DeMint of South Carolina also weighed in, saying, "Here they go again," while describing efforts to revive the regulation as "nothing more than an attempt to muzzle the free speech of conservative Americans." According to McCain, the Fairness Doctrine "had a chilling effect on free speech, and it is hard to imagine that the American people would support reinstating a policy where the federal government would be required to police the airwaves to ensure differing viewpoints are offered." Senator DeMint summed up the conventional conservative wisdom: "We must act now to preserve all Americans' First Amendment rights," he concluded. "If liberals had their way, this unfair doctrine would give the heavy hand of government control over talk radio."

Meanwhile, representatives of the Center for American Progress and the Free Press, whose joint report declared, "right-wing talk reigns supreme on America's airwaves," told the Cybercast News Service that the GOP reaction was the result of conservative talk radio's influence. They noted that their report did *not* call for reinstating the Fairness Doctrine. Instead, their recommendations to "close the gap" between the number of conservative and liberal talkers on the air included increased government regulation and greater diversity of commercial radio station owners.

As CAP senior fellow Mark Lloyd noted, the report concluded that the real issue is "ownership rules that do not serve the public interest." Instead of addressing the ownership issue, said Lloyd, "Fox News and talk radio and Drudge [the Drudge Report Web site] want to shift the focus to the Fairness Doctrine. We'll continue to say that our goal is greater diversity in media ownership."

Democratic politicians such as Wisconsin congressman David Obey claimed the Republican efforts were simply meant to provide talking points for "yap yap TV" and conservative talk show hosts. Channeling the Bard, Obey dismissed the bill as "much ado about nothing" and "sound and fury, signifying nothing."

But to conservatives such as Joseph Farah, the battle—far from being about nothing—was actually about *everything*, or at least everything that mattered: "America is short on leadership right now," Farah opined. "Radio talk show hosts, who every day belt out the truth that no one else in the broadcast world dares to speak, are the closest thing today's Americans have to real leadership. Eliminate talk radio and America goes down the tubes."

The issue of fairness is an ancient *bête noir* for the conservative talkers and their listeners alike, many of whom still harbor deep-seated feelings of exclusion, alienation, and victimization from decades past. In fact, many on the right attribute the very presence of conservatives on the airwaves to the demise of the Fairness Doctrine. Even 20 years ago, many conservatives deemed the rest of what they now term the "mainstream media," including wire services, newspapers, and major broadcast networks, a wasteland of liberal opinion. But AM radio—a technically outdated and largely ignored medium in the early 1980s—represented an instantly accessible market niche, one that allowed conservative talk show hosts to tap into what was seen as a substantial and underserved audience that was angry, white, and largely male. In theory, these listeners decried what they saw as their declining influence in American society, blaming feminists (or, as Limbaugh derisively dubbed them, "feminazis"), homosexuals, minorities, Democrats, and liberals. The neglected AM radio format and its potentially attractive market were ready and waiting for a burst of energy, entertainment, and humor, and soon Limbaugh, and after him a coterie of copycats, began to give the listeners what they seemed to want.

Indeed, given today's new digital media universe, with its countless possibilities for communication beyond those, like radio and television, that require the use of public resources, the Fairness Doctrine may very well be an outmoded solution to an ongoing problem. This "modern critique" is hardly limited to right-wing circles. Columnist Adam Reilly, for example, did a good job of outlining the argument in 2007 in the liberal weekly the *Boston Phoenix,* saying that reverting to the past "would be silly and wrongheaded" and that "in both theory and in practice, the Fairness Doctrine was a bad idea."

Here's why, according to Reilly: "The Fairness Doctrine was the child of a primitive day, when radio bandwidth was limited and television was still developing. Cable TV, satellite radio, and the Internet—and all that it has spawned: e-mail, search engines, blogs, podcasts, YouTube—were beyond conception."

Under the doctrine, Reilly points out, political appointees acted "as policemen of sorts, regulating broadcasters in a way that would be unthinkable for newspapers and magazines. The government was called upon to regulate political discussion, that discussion might ultimately affect government action. There was a circularity to this that was so contradictory as to be ridiculous."

Reilly wrote that he is "thankful" the doctrine died in 1987, when the Reagan-era FCC "rightly concluded that cable and other communication innovations would revolutionize how we generate and consume entertainment and information." Noting that there are "a staggering 14,000 radio stations now broadcasting throughout the nation" and that talk radio accounts for less than 4 percent of the audience, his liberal critique of the Fairness Doctrine concluded that "diversity of opinion in media is not an endangered species," and "there is also no shortage of debate and no deficit of conflicting opinions in the current media landscape. Cable, satellite, and the Internet have not only spawned it, they guarantee it. And as powerful as talk radio is, radio itself is a much smaller and less significant piece of the media constellation today than it was in 1949."

So the notion that the Fairness Doctrine "is an old idea for a time now past," that "it was never a very good idea," and that it's "best left dead and buried" is certainly not limited to the right. Moreover, despite supportive comments by a handful of both Democratic and Republican politicians, including Senators John Kerry, Richard Durbin, Dianne Feinstein, and Trent Lott, as well as Ohio Democratic congressman and erstwhile presidential candidate Dennis Kucinich, the political will to reimpose it is almost certainly lacking.

Still, Feinstein's remarks during an interview by Chris Wallace on *Fox News Sunday* made many conservatives sit up and take notice. "In my view, talk radio tends to be one-sided. It also tends to be dwelling in hyperbole," she said. "It's explosive. It pushes people to, I think, extreme views without a lot of information." When Wallace asked about bringing back the Fairness Doctrine, Feinstein said, "Well, I'm looking at it."

A handful of other Democrats were subsequently more direct. "It's time to reinstitute the Fairness Doctrine," Senator Durbin said. "I have this old-fashioned attitude that when Americans hear both sides of the story, they're in a better position to make a decision." And Senator Kerry, the Democratic presidential nominee in 2004, also went on the offensive. "I think the Fairness Doctrine ought to be there, and I also think the equal time doctrine ought to come back," Kerry told public broadcaster Brian Lehrer. "One of the most profound changes in the balance of the media is when the conservatives got rid of the equal time requirements, and the result is that they have been able to squeeze down and squeeze out opinion of opposing views, and I think it's been a very important transition in the imbalance of our public eye."

Some Republican officeholders—notably Senator Lott—also initially "seemed to suggest that this new talk radio fixation" on the Fairness Doctrine "amounted to uninformed mischief-making," according to *Broadcasting & Cable*. After Lott made harsh comments about talk radio during the immigration debate and was met with fierce opposition, he began to back off his previous criticism of conservative talkers. But historically he had favored the Fairness Doctrine—even opposing efforts by President Reagan and his Republican colleagues to get rid of it in 1987. "We have unfairness now even with the Fairness Doctrine," Lott observed at the time. "Heaven knows what would happen without a Fairness Doctrine."

When pressed 20 years later by Chris Wallace, however, Lott "put the blame on politicians for not making the issue clearer to constituents," as noted in the trade journal. Other Republicans, however, "joined in the rabble-rousing, denouncing the policy as everything from the 'unfairness doctrine' to the 'leftist censorship doctrine.'" Florida's Republican representative Tom Feeney even went so far as to remark that thoughts of returning to it represented a "hallmark of a totalitarian regime."

Perhaps Feeney or someone else in the Republican Party should have tipped off Ohio senator George Voinovich about this imminent fairness fascism. When asked by Sean Hannity about the purported efforts to bring back the Fairness Doctrine, Voinovich showed that he—like many Americans—had absolutely no idea what the ginned-up debate was all about.

"Fairness Doctrine—I'm all for it, whatever it is," Voinovich excitedly told Hannity. "I think everyone should be open to show the other side. That's what you do every night on Fox. That's great!" When Hannity promptly noted that the Fairness Doctrine would establish government regulatory bureaucracies to enforce this balance, Voinovich quickly did an about-face.

Senators Voinovich and Lott aside, there is still absolutely no chance the Fairness Doctrine will return under the current Republican administration. Yet conservatives fear that, post-Bush,

a Democratic-led Congress under a new Democratic president—
having witnessed the defeat of the immigration bill, driven in large
part by talk radio—might one day soon try to resurrect the doctrine.

To conservatives and their supporters, "The War on Talk
Radio" involves numerous types of attacks: "some out in the open,
some behind the scenes. All are intended to throttle talk radio," as
WorldNetDaily.com reported. "Some of the attacks are congressional, such as the controversial 'Fairness Doctrine,'" Joseph Farah
reminded his readers. "Some of the attacks on talk radio are quiet
and technical—like proposals to force minority ownership on radio stations in an effort to get a more left-leaning worldview on
the air...Other attacks are more public and sensational—like the
efforts of Jesse Jackson and Al Sharpton against talk show hosts."

After successfully leading the charge against talker Don Imus
for "using a watered-down version of the coarse language that permeates today's black music industry," Jackson and Sharpton "are
sharpening their knives to go after more talk hosts for 'abuse of
the airwaves,'" said Farah. Still other attacks "are based on charges
of 'bigotry and hate speech.' Currently, Rush Limbaugh, Michael
Savage, Bill O'Reilly, Glenn Beck, Neal Boortz, John Gibson, and
Michael Smerconish have all been declared to be under scrutiny
for their on-air 'hate speech.'"

Backed by this relentless drumbeat, conservatives on talk radio
reacted to the fairness threat—whether real or perceived—quickly
and in force. In short order, the possible return of the reviled
Fairness Doctrine replaced the immigration debate as a chief
topic of right-wing radio scorn. Yet progressives of most stripes
didn't see the return of the Fairness Doctrine as the solution to
their problems either. Instead, they called for the restoration of

both local and national caps on media ownership as well as more local input into licensing decisions and a renewed commitment to enforceable and fair public interest rules. Such proposals, they argued, shouldn't be seen in a strict "left versus right" frame; after all, there are as many issues of concern to conservatives that the media doesn't cover.

Is the right's fear grounded in reality? Might the Fairness Doctrine return if the White House goes to a Democrat? Most leading progressives in and out of the Democratic Party dismiss the possibility. But executives within the broadcast industry are not as dismissive. "I think it is a very real threat," an anonymous veteran TV network executive told *Broadcasting & Cable.* "There are a lot of members on both sides of the aisle who are very upset about the role talk radio played in the demise of the [immigration] bill." News analyst Craig Crawford of *Congressional Quarterly* said, "Unless broadcasters take steps to voluntarily balance their programming, they can expect a return of fairness rules if Democrats keep control of Congress and win the White House next year." Radio-Television News Directors Association president Barbara Cochran added, "RTNDA welcomed the demise of the Fairness Doctrine. We certainly think it would be misguided to try to bring it back at this point." And David Rehr, president and CEO of the National Association of Broadcasters, said in a statement that restoring the rule "would stifle the growth of diverse views and, in effect, make free speech less free.

"Today, there are over 13,000 radio stations, more than 1,700 TV stations, nine broadcast TV networks, hundreds of cable and satellite channels, scores of mobile media devices, and an infinite number of Internet sites that cater to every political persuasion and ideology," Rehr concluded. "Bringing back the Fairness Doctrine is unnecessary, unwarranted, and unconstitutional."

Even assuming there is no return to "fairness," the fact remains that there is a tremendous imbalance in news and current events talk radio today. Shouldn't *something* be done to correct it? As temporary "trustees" of the public airwaves, don't those who hold radio licenses have an obligation "to afford reasonable opportunity for discussion of contrasting points of view on controversial issues of public importance?" [from a letter sent by NAB president Rehr to Congress: http://www.nab.org/AM/Template.cfm?Section=Search &template=/CM/HTMLDisplay.cfm&ContentID=9768]

If so, how is that possible in the current environment, where more than 90 percent of news and current events radio talk show hosts skew conservative? Sole reliance on the marketplace has yet to provide a solution. Can liberals compete with conservatives in attracting both listeners and advertisers? Ed Schultz, for example, regularly outperforms Sean Hannity in Seattle, Portland, San Diego, Denver, Albuquerque, and Miami. But self-identified liberals like Schultz can't compete everywhere unless given the opportunity to do so.

Is the answer somehow to force the marketplace to open up the airwaves and make room for more progressive talk? Many conservatives, such as Oregon's Republican congressman Greg Walden, argue that the predominance of right-leaning radio is a simple case of economics. "It's not my fault Air America went bankrupt," says Walden, another congressional broadcaster whose radio stations carry Limbaugh, Hannity, and Michael Reagan (whose father, President Ronald Reagan, vetoed the doctrine when Congress tried to legislate it).

In any event, it's difficult to deny that the marketplace has failed to police itself and correct an obvious imbalance in radio talk. "Ultimately, of course, the promises of self-regulation have proven ineffective when it comes to the public's airwaves," Josh Silver noted in a post on AlterNet.org. "That's due as much to cultural changes in the industry as anything else; those airwaves once came with a sense of responsibility—an understanding that broadcasters were in some way holding up their end of a public trust—that is increasingly hard to find in corporate America today."

Many progressives have begun turning the tables and proclaiming that the marketplace—and not the government—should prevail. In their view, that's the real reason conservatives are in a state of panic today. Despite their continued dominance and evident influence, progressives argue, conservatives are actually worried about leveling the talk radio playing field, because the so-called free market–loving conservatives are afraid of real competition.

John Moyers, of TomPaine.com, put it well:

"We [citizens] actually own the public airwaves, so we should use that power to challenge radio stations' licenses. Conservative talk radio has been dominant for 20 years, even as politics have shifted back and forth, but the audience is still being underserved. Talk show hosts are now totally consistent with ownership of stations. The owners are conservative, and so is programming. Rush and Sean Hannity are not *real* populists; if they were, they would have a giant audience, because the biggest demographic in America is made up of people who feel powerless, who feel no one stands up for them. They certainly don't speak for the little guy, although they purport to."

A Brief History of Fairness

Heaven knows what would happen without a Fairness Doctrine.
—Trent Lott

The origins of the Federal Communications Commission's Fairness Doctrine date back to the earliest days of broadcasting, its regulation, and government concerns over how best to protect the public interest. When radio was born, stations were originally free to broadcast on any frequency. Soon, however, the radio dial began to fill up and the stations' signals began interfering with one another. In response, Congress passed the Radio Act of 1927, which divided the radio spectrum and issued licenses to broadcast on particular frequencies. The act also set up the FCC's forerunner, the Federal Radio Commission (FRC), and ordered it to issue the licenses so as to ensure that licensees served the "public convenience, interest, or necessity." The following year, the FRC called for broadcasters to show "due regard for the opinions of others," a policy that later became known as the Fairness Doctrine.

The initial rationale behind the creation of the doctrine centered on the relative scarcity of broadcast licenses, which are of course limited to available airwave frequencies. Regulators decided that, in exchange for the exclusive use of this scarce public resource, those who obtained licenses should be required to accept certain obligations deemed to be in the public interest. The Fairness Doctrine was one of those obligations, designed to ensure that a variety of views were heard on the airwaves.

The doctrine, formally adopted as an FCC rule in 1949, required broadcasters to devote "a reasonable percentage of their broadcast time" to the consideration of controversial matters of interest to the public and to air contrasting views about them. A decade later Congress amended the Communications Act of 1934 to incorporate the Fairness Doctrine, noting, "A broadcast licensee shall afford reasonable opportunity for discussion of conflicting views on matters of public importance." Ten years after that, in 1969, the Supreme Court upheld the doctrine's constitutionality (in *Red Lion Broadcasting Co. v. FCC*), leading the FCC ultimately to call the doctrine "the single most important requirement of operation in the public interest—the sine qua non for grant of a renewal of license" (FCC Fairness Report, 1974).

In the Red Lion case, Justice Byron White dismissed charges that the doctrine allowed the government to exert editorial control and thus violate broadcasters' First Amendment rights, noting, "There is no sanctuary in the First Amendment for unlimited private censorship operating in a medium not open to all." Ultimately, the court unanimously found that the Fairness Doctrine actually advanced First Amendment values by safeguarding the public's right to be informed on issues affecting our democracy, while at the same time balancing broadcasters' rights to the broad editorial discretion. But a series of later court rulings seemed to push in another direction...

In practice, government enforcement of the principles that make up the Fairness Doctrine were sometimes applied selectively and were misused for political purposes by Democrats and Republicans alike. President Richard Nixon, for example, who famously accused the media of being hostile to him (his vice president, Spiro Agnew, dubbed them the "nattering nabobs of negativity"), began a systematic campaign to harass radio and television stations he considered unfriendly, according to one Heritage Foundation report. But Nixon wasn't the only president—or even the first—to try to use the Fairness Doctrine to stifle criticism.

Bill Ruder, an assistant secretary of commerce in President John F. Kennedy's administration, explained the way the doctrine was used in the early 1960s, in former CBS News president Fred Friendly's 1976 book *The Good Guys, the Bad Guys and the First Amendment*: "We had a massive strategy to use the Fairness Doctrine to challenge and harass the right-wing broadcasters and hope the challenge would be so costly to them that they would be inhibited and decide it was too expensive to continue," said Ruder. The strategy was developed in 1962 after Kennedy's plan to persuade the U.S. Senate to approve a nuclear test ban treaty was attacked by broadcasters. The Citizens Committee for a Nuclear Test Ban Treaty (established and funded by Democrats) demanded free reply time under the Fairness Doctrine anytime a broadcaster denounced the treaty. The Senate later overwhelmingly ratified it.

Two years later, during the 1964 presidential campaign, Democrats supporting President Lyndon Johnson prepared a kit explaining "how to demand time under the Fairness Doctrine." The result was more than 1,000 letters to stations—and 1,600 hours of airtime. In a confidential report to the Democratic National Committee, Martin Firestone, a former Federal Communications Commission staffer, explained: "The right-wingers operate on a strictly cash basis, and it is for this reason that they are carried by so many small stations. Were our efforts to be continued on a year-round basis, we would find that many of these stations would consider the broadcasts of these programs bothersome and burdensome (especially if they are ultimately required to give us free time), and would start dropping the programs from their broadcast schedule."

In any event, the doctrine did not require that any individual program be balanced, it didn't require that licensees devote equal time to opposing points of view, and it didn't require that a station's overall program lineup be completely balanced. Moreover, it demonstrably was *not* responsible, as Limbaugh and his acolytes repeatedly claim, for preventing conservative talk show hosts from dominating the airwaves, as they have since the doctrine's repeal. In fact, as the liberal watchdog group Fairness and Accuracy in Media reported in 2005, "not one Fairness Doctrine decision issued by the FCC...ever concerned itself with talk shows. Indeed, the talk show format was born and flourished while the doctrine was in operation." And, as noted in an earlier FAIR report ("The Way Things Aren't," Rendall, et al., 1995), "Before the doctrine was repealed, right-wing hosts frequently dominated talk show schedules, even in liberal cities, but none was ever muzzled."

In sum, what the Fairness Doctrine did was simply to prohibit stations from broadcasting any single perspective without ever presenting opposing views. When it was in place, many different citizen groups across a wide political spectrum, including the ACLU, the National Rifle Association, and even the far-right media watchdog group Accuracy In Media (AIM), employed it to expand debate. AIM founder Reed Irvine actually argued that repeal of the Fairness Doctrine would make liberal bias in the media worse. "Many [broadcasters] have done no more than pay lip service to fairness even when it was required by law," Irvine wrote in a letter to the *New York Times*. "It is foolish to think that they would suddenly become addicted to fairness if all legal restraints on their uninhibited exercise of power were removed."

In fact and in practice, the doctrine itself never required "equal time"; often the "fairness" response received far less airtime than did the original perspective it responded to. As FAIR noted, "As a guarantor of balance and inclusion, the Fairness Doctrine was no panacea. It was somewhat vague and depended on the vigilance of listeners." Its greater impact came from "its codification of the principle that broadcasters had a responsibility to present a range of views on controversial issues."

With the 1980s came "the Reagan Revolution" and its emphasis on limited government and deregulation. President Reagan appointed a broadcast industry lawyer, Mark S. Fowler, as the new FCC head. Fowler dismissed the concept that broadcasters bore special responsibilities as trustees of the public interest and held that, as the *Los Angeles Times* reported, "the perception of broadcasters as community trustees should be replaced by a view of broadcasters as marketplace participants."

Fowler and other commissioners, the majority of whom were also appointed by President Reagan, dismissed the findings of the Supreme Court in the Red Lion case and claimed that the doctrine did in fact violate broadcasters' First Amendment rights to free speech. They felt that the doctrine chilled rather than stimulated debate, saying that broadcasters refrained from addressing controversial topics of public interest out of fear of demands for response time and challenges to their licenses.

In response, the FCC stopped enforcing the doctrine before it formally revoked it. Although a majority of the commissioners wanted to repeal it, Congress's 1959 amendment to the

Communications Act had already given the doctrine the force of law. But a 1986 decision by the U.S. Court of Appeals (the majority in the two-to-one opinion came from Judge Robert Bork and then Judge Antonin Scalia, both Reagan appointees on the D.C. Circuit) solved the problem by ruling that Congress had not actually made the doctrine into a law. Instead, the court ruled that the 1959 amendment established that the FCC *could* apply the doctrine but was not *obliged* to. The decision marked the beginning of the end for the Fairness Doctrine. Concluding that it had begun to inhibit political discourse rather than enhance it, the FCC repealed the doctrine in 1987 by a vote of four to zero.

Although the FCC vote was unanimous, opposition to the Fairness Doctrine among conservatives was not. The effort to scrap it was actively resisted by some in Congress, including Trent Lott, who as House minority whip was then the second-ranking Republican in the House of Representatives. Writing in *California Lawyer* magazine a year after the vote, former FCC commissioner Nicholas Johnson addressed attempts to bring the Fairness Doctrine back as "a struggle for nothing less than possession of the First Amendment: Who gets to have and express opinions in America." Though Congress overwhelmingly passed a bill reinstating the doctrine later that year, President Reagan vetoed it, and a later attempt (the one dubbed, in a nod to Limbaugh's primacy, the "Hush Rush" bill) went nowhere after President George H.W. Bush threatened his own veto.

Harrison is the editor and publisher of *Talkers Magazine*, the leading trade publication for the talk radio industry.

A recent report by the Center for American Progress claims that conservatives dominate talk radio.
The CAP report is totally wrong. I would characterize it as a flawed, unscientific survey. The overall talk radio universe includes public broadcasting, urban talk, shock jocks, satellite radio, and news talk radio. Liberals have quite a large chunk of radio, maybe even the same percentage as the right wing.

Did conservative talk radio hosts kill the immigration bill?
You can't make people believe or do something unless they already have a strong feeling and belief in it.

What do you think of the Fairness Doctrine?
The idea of reviving it is the direct product of politicians' annoyance over the immigration bill defeat.

How did you feel when Trent Lott said talk radio was running America?
Trent Lott is stupid; he showed his true colors. There was no problem when the conservative talk radio hosts supported him and agreed with him; then he tried to shut down their speech when they disagreed. Conservative talk radio has power, but it's not a monolithic medium, with a single mind or opinion. Radio is just a tool.

What's the biggest problem in talk radio right now?
It's the dirty secret no one will tell you—that Wall Street has no shame about selling porn and hatred for profit. It's all about greed, not politics....That's the real story—that American corporations will do anything for profit. That's my opinion! So my conclusion is that we as a society must do some soul-searching before looking to blame any one faction...it's an across-the-board thing.

How did this happen?

It really comes down to the fact that there is a *huge* market for hatred, smut, and contentious behavior in America. The media fuels shallow thinking and lowest common denominator tastes for the sole purpose of making profit. The public should be outraged, but they are buying into it instead.

Don Imus has said horrible things before. Why was this time any different?

It was a slow news week. The I-Man is an equal opportunity offender, a bully with a long history of attacking the weak. But they took his shtick out of context and made it look like he's a racist. He should have been fired, but not for the reason that he was.

What do you think of Michael Savage?

Savage is a creep, but a talented creep who makes a lot of money for syndicators and stations. I pity people who believe what he says.

Your magazine just gave him an award for defending the First Amendment.

The award is for defending the First Amendment—not for defending the hideous.

SOUND BITE: Jill Vitale

Jill "Flirty Flipper" Vitale was Sean Hannity's radio producer at WABC from December 1999 to January 2004; she now produces moderate conservative John Gambling's show. Hannity gave her the nickname both because of her dolphin tattoo and because of her propensity for talking to people.

What's the policy for screening callers?

We encourage people who disagree to call up...As long as they're not mumbling, you know, if they speak clearly...If they call up cursing, they don't get on...If they're calling about global warming, we'll put on a little *Twilight Zone* music...It's really funny...Sean used to put on a little hippie music when people were talking about marijuana, stuff like that.

Have you had trouble with guests?

Most of the liberal guests didn't want to go on *Hannity*...On Sean's show there have been crazy debates where guests have hung up. But Sean expects that—he likes debate.

What's Hannity's audience?

We have a lot of FDNY, NYPD, Wall Street, stay-at-home moms, salesmen driving in their cars...It's not one specific type of person, 'cause we get a lot of listeners...They're all—pretty much since 9/11—they're all into protecting the country more. They're stronger on illegal immigration. They seem to be all united on that topic.

How are Gambling and Hannity alike and different?

Both of them are really funny off the air—they're just both kidders, jokesters...Sean's *(best joke)* was...He sent me a live lobster one time 'cause I'm a big animal rights activist...I let it into a freshwater pond...Little did I know that I killed it...People still bring it up around me.

Why are the hosts popular?

I think they're consistent in their beliefs, and they just say it how it is, how they feel—they don't care what other people think. People can sense if you're lying on the air.

You said you were progressive.

I'm for legalizing marijuana. I'm pro-choice. I believe in global warming. I'm an animal rights person. They just take it as a joke—nobody takes me seriously at all. I wish they would. For example, when we had mice around here, the producers put down sticky tape. It's effective, but it's a grueling death, so John and Sean had me on the show. I'm not a good debater...They say I use emotions, not facts. It's all nonmalicious, these guys...They wouldn't know how to hunt a deer if they put it in front of them.

Have the shows influenced you?

I've definitely changed my views on border security and profiling at the airport since I started working here...anything to keep my kids safe...Just from listening to John and Sean's points of view about it and seeing the news about suicide bombers...

Are you surprised that conservative talk is so popular?

It's a little surprising, since so many people disagree with Bush about the war...From what I hear around here, the liberal hosts rant and rave...I don't really listen to Air America, so I just take their word for it.

Greenman, an editor at the *New Yorker* and the author of several books of fiction, wrote a series for the literary publication McSweeney's called "Letters From an Earth Ball," in which a gym ball is subjected to watching and listening to countless hours of Sean Hannity with the high school gym coach. The stories are rooted in real life; between *The Sean Hannity Show, Hannity's America* and *Hannity & Colmes,* Greenman has absorbed more than 1,100 hours of Hannity.

Why Hannity?

Because I don't see an open mind about the world, and that's upsetting. That bluff, take-no-prisoners, Irish dogmatic pose is puzzling to me. You could go a year and never hear a joke. It's a comic strip, in a way, everything is very clear. The lines are thick: "It's the greatest country that God gave the Earth," which may or may not be true, but when you say it a million times, it becomes propaganda. It makes everything seem so simple for a little while. Then, when you turn it off, you realize that the economy *isn't* the best it's been in 20 years.

How is he different from other right-wing talk radio figures?

With O'Reilly, there are certain times where he will side with the ACLU on one crazy issue, and then, when people criticize him for being single-minded, later he'll bring it up. With Hannity, it's simple in all regards; simple as in straightforward and kind of dumb in some ways. He's well prepared, but there's no nuance to the thinking. Limbaugh might seem kind of tricky or strategic; there's a different level of mischief. With Hannity, you could be on a cruise ship with him for 3,000 hours, and I don't think you'd see any more of the real person. It's a very protected persona.

So what's the appeal?

I like argument, and I like people who are angry, and I'm in favor of it in the world. When I was a kid growing up in Miami, there was a curmudgeonly guy named Alan Burke, and it was great. What better thing to do in America than to turn on the radio and listen to an angry person?

Are talk show hosts journalists?

"Journalist" is probably the wrong word, but in their own crazy way they are fact finders and explorers.

CHAPTER 5

Air Wars and Conservative Dominance

Conservative talk radio is not pessimistic, it's optimistic,
it's hopeful for the future. Liberal talk radio is whining and crying,
and nobody wants to listen to that.
—John Gambling, *The John Gambling Show*

I don't know why liberals on talk radio haven't worked yet.
Hollywood has lots of liberals, and we watch their movies, we watch
them on TV. They're smart and good at what they do—
they should be able to figure it out.
—Mike Gallagher, *The Mike Gallagher Show*

In our highly partisan age, one of the few matters that avowed conservatives and liberals appear to agree on is that opinion-oriented talk radio is clearly dominated by voices from the right. They disagree, of course, about the reasons for this disparity, as well as on the need for a remedy, but few if any dispute the overall conservative dominance of the airwaves, at least within the financially valuable, politically influential niche market that news-and-opinion talk radio has become over the course of the past two decades.

A recent report by liberal groups Center for American Progress (CAP) and Free Press spelled out in detail the extent of this dominance. The CAP/FP report, entitled "The Structural Imbalance of Political Talk Radio," examined programming on hundreds of radio stations owned by top programmers. It found that "91 percent is conservative and 9 percent is progressive." The vast majority (236 of 257 stations) fails to broadcast even one minute of progressive talk—and within America's top 10 radio markets, conservative talk tops its progressive counterpart by a more than three-to-one ratio (76 percent is conservative and 24 percent progressive.) Progressive talk is broadcast for two hours or less each weekday in Dallas, Houston, Philadelphia, and Atlanta—four of the top 10 markets.

Industry behemoth Clear Channel, the largest radio station group in the United States (it owns 1,200 stations and boasts more than 110 million listeners) broadcasts 229 hours of progressive talk each weekday—just 14 percent of its programming. CBS Radio, the third-largest group (it owns 144 radio stations, the majority of which are in the nation's top 50 markets), is slightly more balanced—26 percent progressive programming and 74 percent conservative. But fully 99 percent of the programming on the other top groups, including Salem, Citadel (which recently purchased the ABC Radio network), and Cumulus, is conservative.

The overwhelming amount of right-wing radio talk available on America's publicly owned airwaves stands at sharp variance with the political leanings of the overall talk radio audience. Only 43 percent of all talk radio listeners identify themselves as conservative, 23 percent say they are liberal, and 30 percent self-identify as moderate, according to one leading poll. Put another way, *fewer than half* of those listening to talk radio call themselves conservatives.

A look at the nation's leading media market, New York, exemplifies the disparity and the true extent of this conservative domination of the talk radio airwaves. Although metropolitan New York clearly leans left—liberals vastly outnumber conservatives, and New York City's congressional delegation, for example, consists of 12 Democrats and one Republican—the region's right-wing roster of radio talkers mirrors the near-monopoly conservatives enjoy nationwide.

"You'd be hard-put to notice that, though, from listening to the radio," as Hendrik Hertzberg noted in 2003, in an acerbic analysis in the *New Yorker*. "On the AM band, whose low-fidelity signal is perfect for shrill jabber, no fewer than four powerful stations feature 'conservative talk.' Two of them, WMCA and WWDJ, are 'Christian' and heavily salted with attacks on homosexuality, abortion rights, and stem-cell research, and [with] support for school prayer, President Bush's judicial nominees, and Israeli maximalism. The other two pump out a steadier flow of viscous, untreated political sewage.

"The biggie is WABC, which claims the largest talk radio audience in the country," Hertzberg continued. "The station features 15 hours a week of Limbaugh, 15 of Sean Hannity, and 10 of Mark Levin." Advertising dollars from that audience ultimately flowed to one of the largest—and most conservative—media conglomerates in the world. "As its call letters indicate," Hertzberg wrote, "WABC carries the respectable imprimatur of the American Broadcasting

Company, which owns it and provides its hourly newscasts, and, by extension, of ABC's parent company, Disney."

Once upon a time, however, talk radio in New York, as elsewhere, was far more varied, even though the audience and amount of programming was much smaller. Before the industry exploded in the mid-'80s, only 75 stations in the country were all-talk. "Most of them were politically anodyne," as Hertzberg noted. "Conservative hosts were novelty items. Now there are more than 1,300 talk stations, the vast majority of which are relentlessly right wing."

The situation in and around our nation's capital (another apparent liberal bastion) is quite different. In the Washington area— the nation's eighth-largest radio market—conservative talk radio meets with a "cool reception," according to a 2007 *Washington Post* article by Paul Farhi. Many conservative talk programs that rate well elsewhere simply aren't popular in this most political of all towns. With the exception of Rush Limbaugh, whose afternoon program on WMAL remains popular, Farhi found that "conservative talk radio hosts have struggled for years to find a wide audience on the local dial." Bill O'Reilly's nationally syndicated show *The Radio Factor*, for example, was replaced with a sports-talk program. The highly rated Fox News Channel television talker never attracted any sizable radio following in Washington (although in fairness, it must be pointed out that O'Reilly had the misfortune to compete in the same afternoon slot as Limbaugh's show.) But other right-wing talk radio programs, such as those hosted by Laura Ingraham, Glenn Beck, and Michael Savage, have also failed to attract audiences in D.C. In fact, their programs "at times have literally had no ratings in Washington, as measured by Arbitron," according to Farhi, in part "because those hosts are carried on WTNT...a station that has a weak signal, no local programming, and little promotion."

The weak signals, poor lead-in, and lack of promotion sounds all too familiar to many of the progressive radio talkers we spoke with while researching and writing this book. The Washington market is no exception in that regard. Progressive talk station WWRC, which features liberal hosts Stephanie Miller and Ed Schultz, has even lower ratings than WTNT. In fact, as the *Post* article noted, its "audience is so small that it hasn't shown up in Arbitron rankings in years."

Not everyone agrees that the overall radio dial skews conservative, however. Some who contest the notion, such as Michael Harrison, say the statistics claimed by the CAP/FP report are flawed because the "universe" of talk radio programming considered in the study was far too small.

"The CAP report is totally wrong; it just gives the wrong impression. I would characterize it as a flawed, unscientific survey," Harrison said. "The overall talk radio universe includes public broadcasting, urban talk, shock jocks, satellite radio, and news talk radio...So in essence, liberals have quite a large chunk of radio, maybe even the same percentage as the right wing." Nonetheless, he conceded, "It's hard to come up with real figures."

Harrison and other critics of the CAP/FP report like to point to National Public Radio to buttress their arguments. NPR has more total listeners than syndicated conservative talk radio programming. "And it certainly skews liberal," says Harrison. "So conservative talk radio 'domination' is misleading. Yes, it is influential and successful, but it's still just a high-profile niche, one that's only 5 to 7 percent of the total radio audience, and even Rush—who is still clearly the superstar—only gets a portion of that." Harrison's conclusion? "There's a lot more to talk radio than what they call talk radio."

But others argue that, properly viewed, National Public Radio "is an alternative but not an equivalent," as Hertzberg wrote in his *New Yorker* piece. NPR programs like *Morning Edition* and *All Things Considered* are carried on hundreds of stations, just like *The Rush Limbaugh Show*, and their audience "is roughly the size of El Rushbo's—somewhere around 15 million people per week," Hertzberg observed. "But these NPR programs are news-feature broadcasts; they adhere to the practices of journalistic professionalism, including the aspirational ideal of objectivity."

Apart from the fact that the NPR programming is identifiably journalistic and not *entertainment*—as Limbaugh and virtually every other member of the conservative talk radio firmament define and describe their programs—it is also largely free of political commentary. "In contrast, Limbaugh and his scores of national and local imitators aggressively propagandize on behalf of the conservative wing of the Republican Party and the domestic and foreign policies of the Bush administration," Hertzberg noted.

Noncommercial, not-for-profit, government-subsidized NPR aside, even in markets where liberal talk *has* shown itself to be commercially competitive, conservative programming still dominates. As the CAP/FP study notes, "Although there is a clear demand and proven success of progressive talk" in these markets (at least), "station owners still elect to stack the airwaves with one-sided broadcasting." Is the market failing to meet audience demand? When more than 90 percent of the news-and-opinion talk radio programming broadcast each weekday is conservative—despite a demonstrable diversity of opinions among audiences, and given the proven success of progressive shows in some markets—can it truly be said that the marketplace is meeting consumers' desires? If not, why not?

Explanations abound. The two most frequently cited reasons are simple consumer demand and the end of the Fairness Doctrine in 1987. On the demand side, many conservative stalwarts say that the ideas and issues covered on right-wing talk radio simply resonate more with the audience; others claim superior talent and better entertainers are the reason. Some corporate representatives claim the reasons behind conservative talk radio's success are more financial than political, saying it's simply easier to sell ads for conservative talk radio. Others point out (with more justification) that the business models and practices of liberal efforts such as the Air America network (for example) have been severely flawed.

But most conservatives still credit the demise of the Fairness Doctrine with opening up the airwaves to conservative thought, and they fear its return may be imminent. Most liberals, on the other hand, say the Fairness Doctrine has nothing to do with conservative air dominance and has little real chance of ever returning.

Most of the other proposed explanations for the dominance of conservative talk radio, however, don't hold up to close examination. The "our ideas are better and resonate more with the audience" argument is belied by the audience's own political self-identification; remember, less than half the listening audience claims to be conservative. And the "it's-commercial-not-political" explanation, in particular, seems circular and somewhat specious. When Clear Channel in New England dumped its liberal talk format, Clear Channel market manager Mike Crusham explained to the *Boston Herald* that the move was financially and not politically motivated. "I always found, at least in my past life, that it's tougher to sell advertising on progressive talk," he said.

While it's unclear how many past lives Crusham has led, his commercial contention is simply untrue in this one, as evidenced by the many ratings and advertising successes liberal talkers have enjoyed when and where they have been able to compete on an equal footing with conservatives. Radio consultant Donna Halper, who had been pushing to get progressive talk on the air in Boston, argued that the format could work if given enough resources. "It isn't an easy sell," Halper admitted to the *Herald*, then quickly pointed out, "but then again, neither was right-wing conservative talk when it started out."

The conventional conservative and corporate wisdom holds that right-wing talk dominates radio because of the "invisible hand" of an allegedly free market. In fact the inverse may be true; for at least some media conglomerates, advancing a series of political narratives may ultimately be as much in their interest as a single division's healthy bottom line. As the CAP/FP report shows, even in markets where progressive talk has demonstrated its competitiveness, conservative programming still dominates the radio airwaves. As the report's authors note: "[A]lthough there is a clear demand and proven success of progressive talk" in these markets, "station owners still elect to stack the airwaves with one-sided broadcasting." Their inevitable conclusion is that, in radio, the "market" simply isn't meeting consumers' tastes. Conservative talk radio's dominance may owe more to politically created market failure than to any other factor—thus further undercutting the argument that the reasons for this dominance are financial and not political in nature.

Needless to say, an inefficient market isn't the only reason liberal talk shows aren't reaching more audiences and thus attracting advertisers. Running an efficient business, having a clear focus, and producing quality programming also helps a great deal—and the truth is that too often organized liberal responses to conservative air dominance, such as the much-ballyhooed Air America, have failed to do at least some of that. While its corporate woes have been well documented, Air America executives may also have set the entire enterprise up for failure by defining its mission in overtly *political* rather than in *broadcast* or *entertainment* terms, as well as (particularly in its initial phases) relying on inexperienced on-air talent, such as comedians, actors, and celebrities, rather than experienced radio professionals such as Limbaugh.

But as the CAP/FP study details, neither the demands of the marketplace nor the demise of the Fairness Doctrine adequately explain why conservative talk radio dominates the airwaves. Instead, disparities in the amount of conservative and progressive programming seem largely to reflect an absence of localism in American radio markets. This shortfall results from the consolidation of ownership in radio stations and a concomitant dominance of syndicated programming that does not match local community needs. "[T]he gap between conservative and progressive talk radio is the result of multiple structural problems in the U.S. regulatory system, particularly the complete breakdown of the public trustee concept of broadcast, the elimination of clear public interest requirements for broadcasting, and the relaxation of ownership rules, including the requirement of local participation in management," the report concludes. "Ownership diversity is perhaps the single most important variable contributing to the structural imbalance based on the data."

With deregulation and consolidation of radio station ownership meeting neither audience demand nor community needs, what is needed instead, the report's authors argue, is greater localism:

> This analysis suggests that any effort to encourage more responsive and balanced radio programming will first require steps to increase localism and diversify radio station ownership to better meet local and community needs. We suggest three ways to accomplish this: restore local and national caps on the ownership of commercial radio stations. Ensure greater local accountability over radio licensing. Require commercial owners who fail to abide by enforceable public interest obligations to pay a fee to support public broadcasting.

"We want more voices on the radio," Free Press policy director Ben Scott explained. "Our goal is not less speech, it's more speech."

Conservatives tend to use the simple "we're better at this than you are" explanation to explain their air dominance. They like to ask, "Why has there never been a 'liberal' Rush Limbaugh?" The answer, according to *National Review* writer Byron York, is "not terribly complicated," as he explained in his July 2007 article "Why Rush Wins."

"There are plenty of theories to explain his success, along with that of other conservatives who have followed in his footsteps," York begins. Some on the right "argue that conservative ideas are simply superior, so they attract a larger audience." Others, he says, "explain that the liberal audience has more listening choices—NPR, urban radio—so they never rallied 'round a liberal Rush."

York even partially summarizes the argument advanced by the Center for American Progress—"the liberal think tank run by former Clinton White House chief of staff John Podesta"—that takes corporate ownership to task. "Big companies like Clear Channel, the center says, own too many stations on which they broadcast too much conservative talk. If station ownership were more diverse, the theory goes, there would be more liberals on the air, so the center wants the government to force Clear Channel and others to downsize themselves to give liberal talkers a chance."

But in reality, York and other conservative commentators contend, the answer is just not that complicated. Simply put, "Talk radio is radio, and Limbaugh knows more about radio than all his would-be replacements on the left. He's just better at it than they are."

What motivates Limbaugh and his fellow talkers, York declared, is not politics, but *good radio*. This became apparent, York wrote, during a discussion he and Limbaugh had about the years before the repeal of—you guessed it—the Fairness Doctrine. When Limbaugh remembered "being ordered by station management not to discuss controversial topics—pretty much standard procedure at the time—it was clear how frustrating he found the situation," York noted. "But his frustration seemed to come not so much from being forbidden to discuss politics on the air as from being forbidden from discussing anything interesting on the air."

Limbaugh sometimes found himself forced to share the air with community leaders who objected to something he had said.

This made him unhappy—not, according to York, because he was opposed to differing viewpoints, but because he was opposed to bad radio. "The problem with that is that radio is a business," Limbaugh explained. "You bring in people who are not broadcast professionals and give them unchallenged time...You try to make it as stimulating as possible, but..." One could almost hear "Limbaugh's teeth grinding," York said, as he recalled being forced to put on a program that was "dull and boring and horrible."

Bad radio is something Rush simply cannot do, York concluded. "And that is why Rush is Rush. He is deeply, deeply offended by the prospect of boring his listeners. And he has worked for years to develop his rather remarkable talent of keeping them interested for three hours a day, five days a week—all by himself."

Conveniently, according to this line of argument, "the bottom line isn't really about politics, it's about radio," says York. "If Limbaugh were a liberal, we'd probably be talking about why liberals dominate talk radio. So you can talk about ownership and diversity all you want. But the bottom line is that Limbaugh simply knows radio, and what works on radio, better than anyone else in the world. That's why he wins."

Conservative writer Victor Davis Hanson echoes York's argument in the pages of the same issue of *National Review* in an article entitled "All's Fair in Love and Talk Radio." Using the ginned-up controversy over the putative return of the Fairness Doctrine as a starting point, Hanson begins by charging that Democrats such as Dianne Feinstein, who called for a return to devoting airtime to all points of view during discussion of controversial topics, were using "Orwellian logic" and stifling free speech. Then he turned to the real topic at hand. "Talk radio is as much entertainment as political opinion," argued Hanson. "It lives or dies by ratings. Those who master the genre—with off-the-wall jokes, mimicry, satire, and bombast—prosper and get their political message across. Those who can't, don't."

If liberal talk show hosts "like an Al Franken, Jerry Brown, or Mario Cuomo" had succeeded in the marketplace, Hanson opined, "Senator Feinstein would see little need for new laws. And we would probably now be spared the present sour-grapes cries about fairness." He then advanced a theory that has been gaining some currency of late in both conservative *and* liberal circles: "For reasons that are not entirely clear, liberals and conservatives tend to excel in different genres of American media. Most successful political radio talk shows are in fact conservative. On the other hand, humorous political TV spoofs, like Jon Stewart's *The Daily Show*, Bill Maher's *Real Time*, or *The Colbert Report*, tend to have a liberal bias.

"Similarly, the major networks—CBS, NBC, and ABC—are liberal bastions," Hanson continued. "So are most of our motion pictures and documentaries." For good measure, he even threw in references to the "most prestigious and oldest grant-giving foundations—Rockefeller, Ford, MacArthur, and Guggenheim" and "the majority of universities, from the most prestigious, like Harvard, to the largest, such as the California State University system," all, to Hanson's mind, "liberal leaning."

But conservatives need not worry, despite being so desperately outnumbered and outgunned. "The truth is that savvy Americans navigate well enough on their own through our various partisan genres," said Hanson. "Liberals flip through the *New York Times*, tune into NPR on the way to work, and rave about a movie or documentary damning the Iraq war. Conservatives call into Rush or Hannity, check blogs for their news, and watch Bill O'Reilly on cable." Given this "populist" media cornucopia, Hanson wonders what everyone is so worried about. "A radio host requires neither a journalism degree nor political connections. He just needs sheer talent. The unforgiving market—judged by how many turn the dial to your show or call in with questions—alone adjudicates success."

That same unforgiving market should encourage progressives and conservatives alike to embrace new audiences and new forms of communication. "Liberals who profess affinity for the little guy should welcome this prairie-fire revolt against the more highbrow *New York Times*, CBS News, or NPR," Hanson concluded. "Rather than promoting government audit of our opinion media, liberals should master talk radio and cable news. And conservatives should work harder at providing countervoices in Hollywood, on the campuses, and amid the major networks and newspapers. Then let the best men and women win in the free arena of ideas and entertainment."

A somewhat similar "liberals are from Venus and conservatives are from Mars" argument has begun to emerge on the left and has already been partially embraced by some on the right; conservatives naturally dominate talk radio while liberals get the Internet. "The political blogosphere is to the left what talk radio is to the right," as syndicated liberal columnist Ellen Goodman put it. "It is a forceful, sometimes demagogic, message-monger organizing tool for the progressive end of the Democratic Party."

Citing the *New Republic*'s Jonathan Chait, who called progressive Internet activists "the most significant mass movement in U.S.

politics since the rise of the Christian right," Goodman claimed, "They've amplified the antiwar, anti-Bush views, become an alternative fund-raising operation, and linked cyberliberals across the country." She also noted "another, less flattering way in which broadband has followed broadcast and the liberal political bloggers mimic the conservative talk show hosts: the chief messengers are overwhelmingly men—white men, even angry white men."

Ultimately, however, ample evidence suggests that the "real radio war" isn't between females and males, whites and other races, politicians and financiers, or even right and left, but simply between big and small. "Talk radio is blamed—or credited, if you wish—for killing President George W. Bush's immigration legislation. The beast has turned on its friend and bitten him in the (right) rear," Floyd J. McKay, a journalism professor emeritus at Western Washington University, noted on the editorial pages of the *Seattle Times*. "Don't look for retribution, however. The right will not turn on its mouthpiece and refuse to appear on its programs or halt conservative talkers' access to influential leaders. Talk radio and the right need each other, and it didn't happen overnight."

Talk and the angry right are "not about to change—but probably not about to grow, either. The more extreme they become, the less they are a factor in American life," the opinion piece concluded. "Even Limbaugh has lost some of his influence as he is outshouted by imitators. The left cannot and should not copy or regulate them; the real need for broadcast reform is elsewhere."

The reason for conservative domination of the radio airwaves, McKay asserted in echoing the CAP/FP analysis, is domination of the industry by "concentrated ownerships...forcing national programming into markets where local voices once prevailed." As a result of these near-monopolies, "programming is fed from central locations; most stations offer little local content. Syndicated talkers get massive audiences from chains, which set the agenda for local audiences who might like another choice." Arguing about "bigoted talkers or potty-mouth shock jocks obscures the real problem: precious airwaves controlled by a handful of corporations whose only interest is making money," McKay concluded.

In keeping with McKay's analysis, the CAP/FP report's examination of more than 10,000 licensed commercial radio stations found, perhaps unsurprisingly, that stations "owned by women, minorities, or local owners are statistically less likely to air conservative hosts or shows." In contrast, "stations controlled by group owners—those with stations in multiple markets or more than three stations in a single market—were statistically more likely to air conservative talk." Markets that aired both conservative and progressive programming were "less concentrated than the markets that aired only one type of programming and were more likely to be the markets that had female- and minority-owned stations."

The combined news-talk radio format now has more than 50 million listeners per week. With the past decade's relentless emphasis on deregulation and consolidation, local ownership has become increasingly difficult to sustain in many markets. Although advocates of deregulation have long insisted that it inevitably leads to more diverse viewpoints on the airwaves, just the opposite has occurred. This evident failure makes the case for more and better regulation of what is on the public airwaves and ultimately speaks to one of the key issues in media reform—one that most observers on the right consistently fail to acknowledge, namely that radio broadcasts are only possible using tens of billions of dollars' worth of *public airwaves.*

So perhaps the "real war" over conservative domination of the air should not be fought over a strict left versus right divide but instead over the "big versus small" chasm. Certainly there are as many issues of concern to the conservative movement as to their progressive counterparts that Big Media isn't covering.

When it comes to the use of those airwaves, the many promises of self-regulation have proven largely ineffective, as Joshua Holland wrote in 2007 on AlterNet.org. The CAP/FP report, Holland argued, proves that's due "as much to cultural changes in the industry as anything else; those airwaves once came with a sense of responsibility—an understanding that broadcasters were in some way holding up their end of a public trust—that is increasingly hard to find in corporate America today." Combined with three decades of "almost obsessive deregulation," Holland wrote, the radio industry's cultural shift ultimately is the issue that "is among the most important in understanding talk radio's structural imbalance."

Although many conservatives have attacked the CAP/FP report (the Center for American Progress reports that no previous study was met with such "vitriol"), in doing so they have often argued falsely that it calls for the enforcement of the Fairness Doctrine. But, in fact, the study's authors are adamant that the doctrine would not address the issue. What they do call for is a restoration of local and national caps on media ownership (limits on how many stations can be owned by one large firm), more local input into licensing decisions, and a renewed commitment to enforceable and fair public interest rules.

Talk of bringing back the Fairness Doctrine has little to recommend it, other than its near-Pavlovian tendency to make most right-wing commentators apoplectic. Focusing instead on the more important issue of ownership, and the need to limit both how many stations any one corporation can own and how long it can operate them, may in the long run prove more effective—if less fun. But whatever the solution, as liberal talker Bill Press wrote in his syndicated column, "the fact remains: there's a tremendous imbalance in talk radio today, and something must be done to correct it."

Why? Because those who hold radio licenses are—in theory at least—merely temporary "trustees" of the public airwaves. They have an obligation "to afford reasonable opportunity for discussion of contrasting points of view on controversial issues of public importance." When 90 percent of talk show hosts skew to the right, the only answer is to open up the airwaves and make room for more progressive talk.

"Can liberals compete with conservatives in attracting both listeners and advertisers? You bet," asserts Press. "Head to head, for example, Ed Schultz regularly outperforms Sean Hannity in Seattle, Portland, San Diego, Denver, Albuquerque, and Miami. But, of course, liberals can't compete where stations refuse to give them the opportunity."

Can fear of competition be the "real reason" conservatives currently seem in such a state of panic over their continued control of the airwaves? Are they really so worried about leveling the talk radio playing field because they are afraid of battling for audiences in the free marketplace of ideas?

"The Big Talker," as he is known on 1210 WPHT, writes regularly for the *Philadelphia Daily News* and the *Philadelphia Inquirer* and has guest-hosted both Bill O'Reilly's radio program and Glenn Beck's cable television program.

What do conservative talk hosts have in common?

The perception of the hard-core group is that "we are victims." But I am not among them. I am pro-choice, I favor stem-cell research, I'm OK with gays hooking up, and I believe to each his own. Nevertheless I am painted with a broad brush as "one of the wing nuts."

How do you classify yourself politically?

I am libertarian more than anything else, not traditional conservative. Diversity is the name of the game on my show.

What's the difference between your show and other conservative talk radio shows?

I'm not angry—nor is my audience, which is usually half men and half women, mostly white, and skews older and more suburban than most right-wing audiences, which are traditionally more male.

How do you feel about the Imus fallout?

The blowback to offensive speech is so strong that it's even reaching guys like me for using a word like "sissies." That is a proper word choice. No speech of mine crosses the line of hate speech.

Don't you think that terms like "sissification" and "limpwristedness" could be taken as antigay slurs?

"Sissification" simply means weak; "limpwristedness" is not an antigay slur. We have a dangerous climate when people like me get attacked for saying things like that. There's a distinct, chilling effect. I do seventeen and a half hours a week on the air—do I sometimes say something stupid? Of course! But if you don't like it, turn the dial. Let the free market reign.

Gallagher premiered *The Mike Gallagher Show* in 1998, and it's now syndicated on nearly 200 stations nationwide. His program is broadcast on the Salem Radio News Network, which also distributes such other conservative talkers as Hugh Hewitt and Michael Medved.

Why is conservative talk radio popular?
Conservative talk radio is successful because of the formula, and because we got branded as the alternative to MSM [mainstream media]. Rush brilliantly captured the "disenfranchisement" feeling of "I'm an outsider fighting for you," which put the stamp forever on talk radio as the right-wing medium of choice. We're broadcasters and entertainers with strong opinions. But our job is to entertain, to be funny, and to be compelling.

What's the most frustrating charge you've heard against you?
That I make up opinions to drive ratings. We all have a responsibility, and I take it very seriously. I am not a shock jock. But talk radio can be a very volatile format. I do five hours a day unscripted, two local, three national. Every day I say two or three things I later wish I hadn't. I'm labeled a bigot because I don't like Jesse Jackson. In the PC world, you can't say anything about blacks, Hispanic illegals, without being called a racist.

What did you think of Trent Lott's "talk radio is running America" remark?
That was a slimy thing to say—particularly since we had defended him for wishing Strom Thurmond a happy birthday. To people like Trent, we are troublemakers who rile up voters.

Are you and Bush at a crossroads on the immigration issue?
We clearly disagree with the president on illegal immigration, and we told him so when we met with him personally. *(Gallagher and a group of other conservative radio hosts, including Sean Hannity, Laura Ingraham, and Neal Boortz, met with Bush to discuss immigration.)*

Do you want more liberal radio?

I'd love to see more liberals on the air—it would take some of the heat off that's now being directed our way.

Do you get along with liberals?

I'm married to one! Talk about sleeping with the enemy. My wife is a typical liberal bleeding heart. She buys the "vast right-wing conspiracy." She drank the Kool-Aid.

The adopted son of former President Ronald Reagan
and his first wife, Jane Wyman, Reagan hosts the four-hour
Michael Reagan Show, which is syndicated through Radio
America. He also delivers conservative commentary on cable
television networks such as the Fox News Channel.

Why aren't there more liberal radio talk shows on the air?

Because liberals are not fun. Liberals have no sense of humor;
they don't know how to laugh at themselves. The ability to do so
was what made my father so popular.

Some of your colleagues say conservatives dominate talk radio because their on-air talent is better.

That's true—because we are radio people. Air America took comedians and actors and tried to make them professional radio
people. Nobody writes my lines, or Rush's or Sean's.

How much do you rely on listeners who call in?

We spin listeners the way disc jockeys spin records. Here's how
to get on the radio if you call in: tell a great story and make the
host sound like a genius. We don't filter callers because of their
political position. In fact it's more fun to argue with people from
the other side than to delete them.

Why do so many conservative talkers sound so angry?

Michael Savage is really one of a kind. But Rush is not angry. Sean
is not angry, and neither am I. People take us out of context. Look
at what happened to Imus. He was just some 70-year-old guy trying to be hip. The hip-hop culture uses those same terms all the
time. When a white guy does it, he loses his job; when black guys
say the same things, they make millions.

Do you have any liberal friends?

Most of my friends are liberal. My closest friend is Alan Colmes. Poor Alan, he gets hell from both the left and the right, he gets bruised and battered by both sides. Bob Beckel and I are friends as well, and he ran two campaigns against my dad. He's a great guy, he just thinks wrong. But when the shouting is over, we go out to dinner together. That's the problem with America today. The rest of this country just doesn't take the gloves off anymore. The debate has gotten much angrier in the past few years. C'mon...it's not personal!

Ziegler hosts the evening John Ziegler Show on KFI in Los Angeles, one of America's leading talk radio stations.

Why does conservative talk radio dominate the airwaves?

Conservative talk radio is the only medium where someone has the option to articulate a position and then back it up while being challenged. It's the most intellectually rigorous medium by far. The listeners are far more diverse than given credit for; ethnically, for example, the audience is perceived as angry white males. And it does skew that way, but not overwhelmingly. Women and people of color are all a highly underrated part of the audience. Economically, the listeners come from all walks of life. But all of them are highly interested news consumers who feel they are not getting the full truth elsewhere.

Why is there so much anger in talk radio?

Talk radio is the only medium that expresses any emotion at all. The reality is that TV and newspapers do not like anger, but talk radio is immediate and not only allows, but also actually fosters, emotion. If you're not angry, you're not alive.

Do you get along with other hosts?

The number of talk shows hosts I have the respect of is minuscule. I can count them on one hand. They're scoundrels, people not qualified to be taken seriously, court jesters, minstrels. In general people who are stars in this business are not very well informed or truthful.

How do you feel about Rush Limbaugh?

Everyone in this business owes Rush a huge debt of gratitude, but I find him extremely redundant now. I would be bored just repeating Republican Party policies. I am also not a fan of Hannity or Bill O'Reilly. Particularly Bill; he's essentially a fraud. And Sean Hannity? He's also too much of a Republican talking head. I'd like to see him be more open-minded about his positions.

Michael Savage?
He's the only guy on the air angrier than I am. But I wonder how much of it is real. He goes too far on some things; he's not disciplined enough, but he's a real talent.

Mark Levin?
Credible, smart, entertaining, but he has a grating voice.

Ed Schultz?
He's as despicable as Bill O'Reilly. He couldn't make it as a conservative, so he became a liberal: a sellout. Who knows what he really believes?

Stephanie Miller?
She's far too smart to be a liberal. Very funny, my favorite liberal talk radio host.

Do you like talk radio?
I am not a big fan of talk radio. It's still a fraudulent medium in many ways. Most talk hosts are not credible, not consistent, and don't believe what they say or say what they believe. They promise unvarnished truth, but in reality 80 to 85 percent of it's just a show. I enjoy the medium and I think I'm good at it, but it's a horrible business!

Gambling's grandfather and father hosted the radio program *Rambling with Gambling*, which began in 1925; Gambling hosted from 1985 until the show ended in 2000. That year the self-described "moderate conservative" moved from WOR to WABC for the station's New York morning drive.

What changes have you witnessed during your time in talk radio?

Dramatic changes, starting with the elimination of the Fairness Doctrine. Some subject matter, if you spoke against a candidate, he could demand equal time. If there were six candidates, you technically had to have them all on. You've had a freer point of view since then.

What would happen if the Fairness Doctrine were reinstated?

It'll decimate talk radio. I'm a conservative, and I would have to open my show up to liberals. It would hamper my success.

What does conservative talk radio give its listeners?

It's optimistic, it's hopeful for the future. The liberal conversation is much more pessimistic, much more negative. If you watch or read the mainstream media, they are predominately leaning toward the liberal point of view. *NBC Nightly News* is frightening and so is the *New York Times*.

Are you saying news organizations can't be objective?

Totally impossible. Can't be done. You can have representatives of different points of view, but you yourself can't be objective. You have therefore colored the news that you're reporting.

What do you think of the charged language used by hosts like Michael Savage and Neal Boortz?

It's a business decision. They get a reaction, it works for them.

What's the future of conservative talk radio?

It's only gonna get bigger and brighter, and it's only gonna get better and better.

Even if a Democrat becomes president?

Even more so. Politics is never-ending. It's like a river, always flowing. It always gives us something to talk about.

CHAPTER 6

Progressive Alternatives

We are an equal-opportunity, pro-choice, antiwar, nonsmoking,
nonsectarian network with a 50–50 male-female staff that recycles.
Always remember to buckle up for safety!
—from Bruce McCall's
"Liberal Radio Network Employment Application"

The unquestioned conservative control of the talk radio airwaves during the past two decades undoubtedly contributed to a string of Republican electoral successes, culminating in the disputed presidential contest of 2000. Following the election of George W. Bush—or his "selection" by the Supreme Court, as many embittered liberal Americans still regard it—progressives finally began to focus their attention on the imbalance in the media and its effect on the electorate. Left-oriented media watchdog groups like Media Matters for America sprang up and began monitoring conservative talkers' every utterance; more policy-minded groups such as Free Press and the Center for American Progress starting publicly examining issues of deregulation and consolidation, corporate media, and the structural reasons underlying conservative media's success. At the same time, a number of progressive activists began pushing for a direct challenge to right-wing air dominance.

Could liberals compete with conservatives in attracting both radio listeners and advertisers? There was some evidence they could, but the lack of a level playing field or an equal opportunity to reach audiences had long made the argument largely theoretical. Liberal talk of right-wing "fear of competition" made conservatives smirk. The lack of any organized progressive response to the conservatives' on-air clout seemed only to bolster claims that their issues and concerns resonated more with audiences, or that right-wing talk radio superstars were simply "better entertainers" with God-given talent superior to that of any liberal who managed to beat the odds and make it onto America's airwaves. The unbalanced ten-to-one ratio of conservative to progressive talk on the radio wasn't *caused* by decisions made in corporate suites, conservatives argued; instead those decisions were *driven* by the success the "better" right-wing talkers had demonstrated in attracting listeners and thus advertisers. News-and-opinion talk radio was stuck in what was either a virtuous or a vicious cycle, depending on your political perspective.

Enter Sheldon and Anita Drobny, a husband-and-wife team of entrepreneurs from Chicago. In late 2002, upset that their favorite liberal radio host, Mike Malloy, was no longer on the local airwaves, the Drobnys decided to try to get Malloy syndicated nationally over the airwaves. (Malloy had worked at WLS in Chicago from 1996 until 2000; his program was then available between October 2000 and February 2004 on the I.E. America Radio Network, which attracted a mostly Internet-based audience.) The

Drobnys asked for assistance from an experienced radio executive named Jon Sinton.

Sinton explained that getting a single progressive program into national syndication would be very difficult; instead he suggested that the Drobnys create a *network* that could offer stations a range of progressive talk programs. They decided to hire Sinton as CEO for an entity called AnShell Media, and they began raising money to create such a network. A few months later, AnShell's intentions were announced in a *New York Times* article entitled "Liberal Radio Is Planned by Rich Group of Democrats." The article pronounced the effort to be "the most ambitious undertaking yet to come from liberal Democrats who believe they are overshadowed in the political propaganda wars by conservative radio and television personalities."

It was true, as the *Times* noted, that previous liberal radio talkers had not fared well. One nationally syndicated program starring former Texas agriculture commissioner Jim Hightower, which Jon Sinton had helped start, didn't gain much traction; another effort featuring former New York governor Mario Cuomo also failed. But now, faced with continued right-wing dominance of talk radio, coupled with the rise of the Fox News Channel and the Republicans' ascendancy in Washington, it appeared that wealthy Democrats would begin putting their money where they wanted liberal mouths to be.

The new venture, Sinton told the *Times*, would seek to disprove not only those who doubted liberal hosts could make it in radio but also those who believed that success in radio required an alliance with one of the handful of major distributors or station groups. "The object of the programming is to be progressive and make a statement that counters this din from the right," Sinton said. "But we have a solid business plan that shows a hole in the market." The market gap Sinton referred to, of course, was the underserved audience of tens of millions of liberal radio listeners. Still, many radio executives refused to believe liberal radio could ever become good business.

Kraig T. Kitchen, chief executive of Premiere Radio Networks, one of the nation's largest radio syndication arms, was among them. An admitted conservative, Kitchen said he would have pursued liberal programs had he thought there was money in them, but he felt that liberal hosts present issues with too much complexity to be entertaining. "It's very hard to define liberalism, unlike how easy it is to define conservatism," Kitchen told the *Times*. "So, as a result, it doesn't evoke the same kind of passion as conservative ideologies do." Sinton countered that liberal attempts such as Hightower's had failed largely because they were out of place in programming schedules otherwise filled with conservatives. "It is very hard to succeed when you throw liberal programming between bookends of Rush Limbaugh and Sean Hannity," he said. "That violates expectations of the listener."

Fund-raising and planning for the new venture continued throughout 2003. Sinton met frequently with comedian Al Franken, an Emmy-winning *Saturday Night Live* writer and the author of *Rush Limbaugh Is a Big Fat Idiot*, in the hopes of convincing him to become the network's anchor talent, while simultaneously trying to lure other personalities, such as actress Janeane Garofalo and *Daily Show* cocreator Lizz Winstead. Meanwhile, the Drobnys found fund-raising difficult. Former Clinton chief of staff John Podesta then introduced them to David Goodfriend, a young lawyer with supposedly rich friends. Goodfriend in turn introduced them to his college roommate Evan Cohen, who was allegedly worth millions. In short order, AnShell Media was sold to Cohen and a partner. The new company was named Progress Media and Cohen was named chairman; Sinton remained as president of programming.

By year's end, the nation's first real progressive talk radio network was close to launch. *New York Times* reporter Jim Rutenberg chronicled its progress once again: "A Democratic investment group planning to start a liberal radio network to counterbalance conservative radio hosts like Rush Limbaugh says it is close to buying radio stations in five major cities," Rutenberg wrote on December 1. "The acquisitions would represent a major move toward making the network real. After its conception was announced in February, many radio analysts and even some Democratic activists predicted that the network would face too many challenges to get off the ground, including finding stations to run its programming and bucking a historical record replete with failed liberal radio attempts."

Progress Media executives told Rutenberg that "they would have the network running by early spring, in time to be part of the public dialogue during the presidential campaign season." The stations the company was said to be acquiring reached listeners in New York, Los Angeles, San Francisco, Philadelphia, and Boston, five of the 10 largest media markets. "We're steady as she goes to have a broadcast debut in early 2004, which gives us time to be part of the election year," said Mark Walsh, an Internet entrepreneur formerly with America Online who had become Progress Media's chief executive. Progress Media, Rutenberg noted in the *Times*, "would not say which stations it was planning to buy," nor "how much the stations would cost altogether." But a major-market station, he concluded, "can cost on the order of $30 million."

As it turned out, the Air America Radio Network, as the new venture was dubbed, launched on March 31, 2004—before any stations had been purchased. So that the nascent network would at least have a presence in the nation's leading media markets, a deal was struck to lease stations such as New York's WLIB. As the nation's only all-progressive talk radio network with a robust on-air presence (the previously anemic United Auto Workers' I.E. America Radio Network, home to hosts such as Mike Malloy and Thom Hartmann, had closed shop just weeks before), Air America soon became the fastest-growing network of any type in modern radio history, gaining 100 affiliated stations, including 18 in the top 20 markets, in just six months.

The night before it went on the air, the network threw a $70,000 launch party, where more than 1,000 guests drank red, white, and blue vodka cocktails while toasting the network's challenge to the dominance of conservative talk radio. The gala did a great job both of promoting Air America and obscuring the fact that the company was already running out of money. Although Progress Media executives had said the company's capitalization was $30 million at launch, that claim proved to be false. (The actual figure was closer to $6 million.)

Just two weeks after launch, contract disputes involving bounced checks led to the loss of stations in two key markets. Two weeks after that, CEO Mark Walsh left the network. Chairman Evan Cohen and his investment partner were forced out a week later by the remaining investors. As part of the reorganization, another new company was formed, and a decision was made *not* to buy any radio stations. After all, within just six weeks, creditors were already owed more than $2 million.

Soon the story of Air America's financial woes began to leak out, and suddenly the publicity wasn't so good anymore. "Five months before a presidential election, Air America should be on a roll," the *Wall Street Journal* noted in a June 21, 2004, front-page story. "Instead, it's grappling with a financial crisis. Creditors are lined up at the door, and it is off the air in two big markets, Los Angeles and Chicago." The paper quoted Rick Cummings, president of the radio division at Emmis Communications, one of the nation's biggest station owners, as saying that the new network's owners had "quickly realized there were a lot of things they didn't know, and one was how to do radio." And that of course was the conventional wisdom: "radio people" (Jon Sinton aside) didn't create Air America, "political people" did. "And radio people will tell you it's all about format," explained Doug Kreeger, who took over management of the network in the wake of the reorganization. "We were trying to defy all conventional logic by putting on progressive programming in a medium that had long been dominated by the right."

Despite the many problems in the executive suites, out on the streets, Air America *was* making an impact in a volatile, highly partisan presidential election year. Even in the face of its financial difficulties, the network succeeded in branding itself as a progressive talk radio alternative and was soon mentioned in the same breath as other leading media brands. "Air America had a big impact," said Kreeger. "Its real strength was that, for the first time, people from a progressive standpoint had their own space. There were no phony talking head 'debates' where progressives were just shoehorned in between conservatives and not really given voice. That was significant." Despite intense scrutiny and little in the bank, Kreeger succeeded in stabilizing the project and increasing distribution. "We came really close to electing a president in 2004," he recalled ruefully in a 2007 interview with us. "Air America was there when nobody else was—and even today, there is no real countervailing choice to conservative domination of the airwaves."

By the end of 2005, the chaos in finances had spread to the programming department, as yet another CEO, Danny Goldberg, broke up the network's morning drive-time show *Morning Sedition*, over Jon Sinton's objections, and let cohost Marc Maron's contract lapse. Maron's last show came on December 16; Goldberg announced *his* resignation less than four months later, after a little more than a year on the job. Janeane Garofalo left a few months later, with the network in increasingly obvious disarray.

By August 2006, when nighttime host Mike Malloy was fired, the irony seemed complete: the whole effort had originally been spurred by the Drobnys' desire to advance Malloy's program. Other Air America on-air talent, including Randi Rhodes, criticized the firing, as did many listeners, who mounted an online campaign, including a petition that gained thousands of signatures, to bring Malloy back. Despite the outpouring of support, Malloy never returned. He moved instead to Nova M, another progressive radio network fledged by the undaunted Drobnys.

In October, Air America filed for bankruptcy, undone by financial shenanigans and apparent deceit; at that point, the company had more than $20 million in liabilities and less than $5 million in assets. Furthermore, it had lost more than $9 million in 2004,

$19 million in 2005, and an additional $13 million in 2006. Air America's spectacular financial flameout seemed only to buttress the long-held and oft-expressed conservative contention that liberal talk radio simply couldn't work. But it seems more likely that the failure resulted from a toxic combination of undercapitalization, incompetence, and borderline criminality on the part of top executives such as Evan Cohen.

The first iteration of Air America was successful in branding and in attracting audiences. At the very time that controversy was swirling in its executive offices, Air America's ratings nationwide averaged a respectable 1.2 audience share in most markets where it was available, according to Arbitron ratings figures. In many markets it fared even better. In Portland, Oregon, it achieved high listenership on station KPOJ, which ranked second among AM stations and sixth overall.

Other markets with good ratings included Seattle and Madison, Wisconsin, where a decision by WXXM station owner Clear Channel to switch away from politically progressive programming to all sports (via Fox Sports) was met with an uproar. WXXM station executives predictably said that money was the issue, not politics. Despite good ratings for progressive talk, they believed more money could be made with a sports format—even one with lower ratings—since it would cost less to produce and ostensibly be an easier sell to advertisers. Jeff Tyler, Clear Channel's Madison market manager, said advertisers stayed away from the station because they opposed the format and that, while the station was making money, it consistently ranked last in reported earnings. Tyler claimed that liberal talk programming faced similar problems nationwide.

Others weren't so convinced. "I'm wondering if the switch to Rupert Murdoch's Fox Sports means the liberal station was more successful than certain people wanted," one listener wrote in a local newspaper. And progressive talk host Ed Schultz, whose show is heard daily on more than 100 stations, blasted Tyler for what he called a failure to turn high ratings into ad sales. "This is not a ratings issue, because the station is number one in Madison. It's an issue of management," Schultz said. "Instead of changing the format, maybe we ought to change Jeff Tyler." Tyler said the company was exploring ways to continue progressive talk in Madison, including picking up liberal hosts on one of its other five local stations. "Our company sales team embraced the station, the format and enthusiasm we all had for the station, and its role in our community," he said. "However, there are many advertisers, local and national, who have been at conflict with the programming or stay away from controversial programming."

Following weeks of public outcry and denunciations from leading politicians, such as Mayor Dave Cieslewicz and U.S. Representative Tammy Baldwin, Clear Channel/Madison announced that it had dropped its plans to switch to an all-sports format. Instead, executives decided to retain the liberal talk format, thus allowing Air America Radio, Ed Schultz, and Stephanie Miller to remain on the air in Wisconsin's capital, on one of the top-rated liberal talk stations in the country.

Clear Channel's Jeff Tyler put the best possible spin on the embarrassing turnaround. "We are overwhelmed by the recent outpouring of support for our progressive talk format from the public, some of our community leaders, and some dedicated local advertisers," he said. "We deeply appreciate the local business leaders who are pledging their advertising support; they are playing an enormous role in helping to keep progressive talk on the air in our community." According to the Liberal Talk Radio blog, Tyler said he hoped to improve the quality of local shows and was encouraged that Air America would do the same for its programming when it emerged from bankruptcy. "We're here to make it work. We're going to put all of our resources into it," he said. "People have spoken out in Madison and said, 'This is a great radio station and we support it.' We encourage them to prove it."

"Air America, for all its faults, gave the progressive talk format a leg up," said Doug Kreeger, looking back at his tenure. "We helped strengthen people like Ed Schultz and Stephanie Miller—and when Clear Channel later began building its own successful progressive talk format, it was a validation of our whole approach. Progressive talk will always be in the marketplace now as a format, and that alone is a huge success."

Buoyed by the evidence that liberal talk resonated with radio listeners in at least some markets, a new investment team surfaced to take Air America out of bankruptcy. In March 2007, the company was purchased for $4.25 million by Green Family Media, made up of New York real estate investor Stephen L. Green and his brother Mark, a Democratic Party activist and former public official. The Greens had already been involved with Air America; Stephen had provided interim financing, and Mark, the former New York City public advocate and past candidate for senator, mayor, and state attorney general, had been a program host. Mark Green told the press the sale would usher in a new phase for Air America focused on digital content distribution like Internet programs and podcasts in addition to radio. "In this digital era, the tech changes by the day, and Air America Radio has to become something of a new-media company," Green said.

A new lineup was unveiled and a new head of programming was named: radio veteran David Bernstein, onetime program director at New York radio station WOR. Bernstein seemed to have a different and broader vision of Air America than its founders. While acknowledging that being a liberal network is a crucial part of Air America's value, he added that he didn't want to hear talk about "energizing the base," as one often did on conservative talk stations. "I don't think of Air America in those terms," Bernstein told the *New York Daily News* in 2007. "I don't see our purpose as 'answering' conservative radio or Rush." Kreeger agreed, at least in part. "The progressive audience and other, independent-minded listeners, are not interested just in being screamed at all day long," he said. "Right-wing talk radio is about a man in a booth screaming and doing diatribes on the attack message of the day. Progressive radio was never about duplicating that format for left-wing people. The 'radio people' thought that a left-wing version of Rush Limbaugh would sell—but the progressive audience wants a different sound—with different voices and information."

In March of 2008, Charlie Kireker, leading a new group of investors, acquired majority control of Air America, with intentions of expanding both the reach and strength of the radio network and building a meaningful interactive business around progressive content. Kireker's 30-year career spans journalism, politics, public policy, and venture capital finance, making him well suited to leading an entrepreneurial company through a phase of expected rapid growth. Kireker and his colleagues believe that a pendulum swing of a 30-year cyclical nature has begun in American politics and that Air America has developed enough of an audience and brand identity to contribute to the flowering of a new progressive tide in the United States.

Despite the missteps thus far, the newly relaunched version of Air America 2.0 has a reasonable chance of surviving and perhaps even thriving, particularly if it can meet its goal of providing smart content and distributing it better. Since the "extreme makeover" of AAR is still very much a trial in progress, the jury of listeners is still out. But new management has again revamped the schedule and promised to deliver "talk radio that's informative, opinion-ated, entertaining."

Of course, there's much more to liberal talk radio than just the Air America network. The number, quality, and stature of pro-gressive alternatives to Limbaugh and his ilk have been mounting steadily in the past few years—no doubt as a result of the rise and resonance of progressive values. One good source of information on the changing playing field is *Talkers*' annual "Heavy Hundred" list of the most important of America's more than 5,000 talk show hosts. Although Limbaugh, Hannity, and Savage top the list, pro-gressive talker Ed Schultz ranks eighth. According to *Talkers*, Schultz (who is syndicated nationally by the Jones Radio Networks) is the "leader of the progressive talk show pack," and his momentum is building fast. He is joined in the top 20 by Fox News Radio's Alan Colmes. Other liberals among the top 40 include Thom Hartmann at 23, Stephanie Miller at 28, and Randi Rhodes at 40. Lionel, who recently joined the Air America 2.0 team, is also near the top of the second tier, ranked 31st.

Other top progressive talkers in the "Heavy Hundred" include Diane Rehm, National Public Radio's popular public affairs host, ranked 94th; and Bill Press, syndicated nationally by Jones Radio Networks, ranked 96th. Rehm's NPR colleagues Neal Conan and Terry Gross are among those ranked in the second *Talkers* tier under the "Heavy Hundred," along with the Nova M-distributed Mike Malloy and Rachel Maddow of Air America.

Although there are now more progressive talkers than ever—and more people listening to them—when it comes to ranking talk show hosts according to the size of their audience, conservatives still clearly rule. The *Talkers* list of "Top Talk Radio Audiences" shows that Limbaugh still reigns supreme, with an estimated average audience of 3.4 million listeners in a quarter hour and a cumulative weekly audience of 13.5 million. Sean Hannity is close behind in audience size with 12.5 million weekly listeners, followed by fellow conservatives Savage, Beck, Ingraham, Boortz, Levin, Mike Gallagher, Michael Medved, and O'Reilly, whose average weekly audience of more than 3.25 million is matched by Ed Schultz. Although estimable, Schultz's audience size is still roughly one-quarter of Limbaugh's. The only other progressive talkers who are heard by at least 1 million listeners each week are Fox's Alan Colmes, Stephanie Miller of Jones Radio Networks, Diane Rehm of NPR, and Air America's Thom Hartmann, Randi Rhodes, and Lionel.

In addition to this nationally syndicated and locally broadcast commercial programming, and the noncommercial NPR programming, other sources of progressive talk are now available to the discerning listener. One example is Nova M Radio, the upstart syndication service originally operated by Sheldon and Anita Drobny as they continued, post–Air America, to pursue their dream of broadcasting progressive talk radio, particularly programs hosted by Mike Malloy and Jeff Farias. The network also airs outside syndicated programming, such as Stephanie Miller, Bill Press, and various Air America Radio programs, including that of Jon Elliott, Rachel Maddow, and others. There are also several excellent progressive talkers, such as the West Coast's Peter B. Collins, who, while not nationally syndicated, are regionally available and reach millions of potential listeners. Most of the hosts chronicled in this book can also be heard on the Internet and on satellite radio.

One would be remiss not to mention the work of Amy Goodman and her colleagues, whose combination radio/television program *Democracy Now* has become a vital source of news and information in progressive circles. The flagship program of the Pacifica Radio network, *Democracy Now* airs on more than 500 radio and television, satellite, and cable TV outlets. Although ideologically opposed, Goodman and her top conservative counterparts share a savvy appreciation for amplifying and echoing their radio presence in other media. Goodman is the author of several bestselling books and writes a widely syndicated newspaper column. Her genuine and growing popularity belies the notion that there is little audience for progressives on radio, but since her program is truly journalistic in nature and doesn't really fit into the talk show genre, she and her work are not considered in depth here.

Even independent, community-based media can attain a sizable audience niche, especially now that new, full-power, noncommercial FM radio stations are available as never before to nonprofit community groups. As the late George Gerbner, dean of the Annenberg School for Communication, once noted, there is still a need for media not run by "corporations that have nothing to tell and everything to sell." And as Goodman herself wrote in one syndicated column, "Community radio is the antidote to that small circle of pundits featured on all the networks, who know so little about so much, explaining the world to us and getting it so wrong. On community radio, you can hear your neighbors, you can hear people from your community: the silenced majority, silenced by the corporate media."

Despite the many and increasing listening options, it is clear that conservatives still overwhelmingly dominate the overall field of talk radio—if not in terms of importance, then certainly in terms of overall audience reach. The question as to why—politics, philosophies, finance, talent, "multiple structural problems in the U.S. regulatory system," or any of the other theories considered in this book—remains open. But at least the argument, at long last, has begun, and the battle to open up the public airwaves is being fought.

Liberal Radio Network Employment Application

By Bruce McCall
Originally published in the New Yorker, *March 29, 2004.*

We are an equal-opportunity, pro-choice, antiwar, nonsmoking, nonsectarian network with a 50–50 male-female staff that recycles. Always remember to buckle up for safety!

Personal Information:

DO NOT WRITE IN THIS SPACE

We respect your civil rights and your right to privacy, and do not ask you to reveal any personal information. We rely on the honor system to inform us if you are a pervert, terrorist, or carrier of mad-cow disease.

1. **Which statement below is incorrect?**
   (a) Ann Coulter is not an evil person.
   (b) There is no need to raise one's voice when arguing a political position.
   (c) We must always remember that Abe Lincoln was a Republican.
   (d) It's important to respect opinions that are different from one's own.
   (e) Nobody is right all the time.
   Answer: Maybe no statement is incorrect.

2. **You're at a Peter, Paul and Mary reunion concert when a right-wing militiaman bursts into the hall with an AK-47 and declares that he will hold everyone hostage until the U.S. government admits to war crimes against patriots and agrees to pay $1 billion in reparations. Do you:**

 (a) Defuse the situation by asking the audience to join Peter, Paul and Mary in singing "If I Had a Hammer."
 (b) Confront the militiaman, and ask to see his gun permit.
 (c) Take up a collection among the audience to pay a token reparation.

 Answer: Perhaps none of the above? Instead, why not call a town meeting and have a free and open debate?

3. **It would not be nice for a liberal radio network commentator to mention:**
 (a) Strom Thurmond's daughter.
 (b) Trent Lott's abrupt comedown.
 (c) Halliburton's overcharges in Iraq.
 (d) George W. Bush's military record.

 Don't know__ Not sure__ Let me think__

4. **It would be nice for a liberal radio network commentator to mention:**
 (a) The eradication of polio.
 (b) UNICEF Christmas cards.
 (c) The bald eagle's comeback.
 (d) Increased car safety.

 I think so__

5. **If Rush Limbaugh were to call me a fuzzy-minded élitist knee-jerk bleeding-heart liberal sissy without cojones enough to support the death penalty, I would:**
 (a) Softly weep.
 (b) Admit that he has a point.
 (c) Ask what the ACLU would do.

 Answer: All three could work.

6. **If I hosted a liberal radio network talk show, my guests would include:**
   (a) Pat Buchanan   (c) Bill O'Reilly
   (b) Pat Robertson   (d) Karl Rove
   (*If you checked none of the above, memorize the "Tolerance 'R' Us" poem posted in every liberal radio network restroom.*)

7. **From the list below, circle your five favorite words/phrases/names:**
   (a) Volvo   (g) Henry Wallace
   (b) Ginseng   (h) Dog bandana
   (c) Berkeley   (i) Tim Robbins
   (d) Canada   (j) Sesame Street
   (e) Hiking   (k) Dobro
   (f) Egg toss   (l) Vietnam

8. **The four funniest moments in PBS history, in my opinion, were:**

   1._____   2._____

   3._____   4._____

If you cannot think of even one, perhaps we should delete this question from the application. What do you think?

Constitutional expert, historian, and author Thom Hartmann began broadcasting from Portland's KPOJ in 2005 and was picked up by many Air America affiliates following Al Franken's departure. He broadcasts six hours a day in the company of his wife and producer, Louise.

You have a very smooth style. We've never heard you get ruffled or shrill.

When you know your material and you're comfortable with it, it's fairly difficult to get rattled. I don't trash people. This is a lesson I learned from growing up with a conservative Republican father. I learned from him how to have a disagreement without being disagreeable.

You often have people on your program who have contrarian views.

I start with the assumption that the person I'm debating wants the same thing I do at the end of the day: a better country and a better life. Where we differ is how we're going to get there. Politics as gladiator sport—my team, your team, shouting each other down—is how it's done on Fox News. I think it's destructive. It teaches people how to fight and argue but not how to understand.

But it seems almost impossible to find common ground.

Conservatives and liberals have a fundamentally different worldview. They have a different understanding of the nature and role of humans in the world relative to each other and to the planet. Once you understand that, then all these different positions on the issues start making sense. My goal is to help my listeners understand how these worldviews inform the debate so they have a better tool kit for interacting with the conservatives in their lives. At the end of the day, you still work in the cubicle next to the guy, or he's still your brother-in-law, or in my case, your dad. You still love each other and respect each other, or can get along and go out and have a beer afterward. I think we need that in America.

SOUND BITE: Thom Hartmann

Let's look at the difference between radio and television.
Radio is the most intimate of all mediums. It is right here in your ear. It's a phone call. Radio is me talking to you. When I'm doing radio, I'm thinking not of 2 or 3 million people; I'm talking to one person.

People can't seem to agree if progressive radio is going to collapse or thrive.
Progressive talk radio has just begun to find an audience. We're at that point where conservative talk radio was when Rush was just starting to catch his stride and some of the imitators or additions to the genre started coming along. The next step is, you're going to see talent breaking out into the larger mainstream of talk radio and not be called progressive or liberal talk radio, but simply be called good talk radio that engages people. We've got a long, long way to go, and we're going there fast.

SOUND BITE: Cenk Uygur

Former lawyer Cenk Uygur is host of Air America's progressive morning drive show, *The Young Turks*.

You used to be a Republican. What happened?
Charles Barkley once said, "I used to be a Republican until they went nuts." When I was growing up in New Jersey we were "moderate" Republicans. Now one wonders whether that's even possible.

How are progressive and conservative audiences different?
I'm biased, but it seems to me the liberal audience is far more educated. You get answers and questions that get into the details of the story, whereas on a conservative station you'll get a caller who says, "You schmuck! You hate the country!" You rarely get an intelligent, well-thought-out question.

Conservative audiences seem so angry.
There are plenty of angry people on the left. I get angry, too. But a lot of the callers will simply agree with conservative hosts, nine out of ten times. On a liberal station audiences are not robots, they are listening to what you're saying, processing it, and then disagreeing with you. That's why Rush calls his listeners "ditto-heads," because they're supposed to agree with him. *Young Turks* listeners don't take a position simply because I take it.

Do you worry about being unscripted?
When you talk for three hours a day unscripted, you're definitely gonna say something stupid. That's what makes it interesting.

How do you feel about Glenn Beck and Laura Ingraham?
I try not to listen to talk radio that much. The people on the other side are either terrifically dull or deranged.

How is it that Hannity, Savage, and Limbaugh are so popular?
Sean Hannity has a huge institutional machine working for him. Savage is entertaining because there is an excellent chance that he has lost his mind. Limbaugh's not as entertaining as he used to be because he's become a Hannity-like walking, talking robot.

Are any of these people different in real life?
Everybody's more polite in real life. I've never had an unpleasant interaction with any of them, and then you listen to them on the radio and think, "Wow, I can't believe that!"

Does the fact that more than 90 percent of talk radio is conservative discourage you?
No, it encourages me. When we started, 99 percent of talk radio was conservative.

British-born American journalist Flanders hosts *RadioNation with Laura Flanders*, weekends, 7:00 to 10:00 p.m. on Air America. Founding director of the Women's Desk at the media watch group FAIR, Flanders produced and hosted *CounterSpin*, FAIR's nationally syndicated radio program for more than 10 years.

Why aren't there more women in talk radio?
The job of talk radio host has largely been limited to being a boy's club, due to an institutional and historical bias. And there's a style to the talk radio format that is stereotypically male. There are some women—notably Randi Rhodes—who do very well with that format. But frankly, it's not the style most women will choose. It's safe to say that women are generally not so confrontational and provocative, but talk radio largely *is*, which is why I say the format itself is, basically, typically male.

What is your approach to callers?
I have no litmus test as to whether they agree with me politically or not. I think part of my job is to talk to anyone. But oddly I found that a large part of my audience doesn't like it when I talk to people from "the other side." That's frightening to me, because I think it's vital for our democracy and society that we encourage open, civil, democratic discourse.

That's not the nature of our politics at the moment, however.
Well, we are in politics when we're doing political talk radio, and not just in "the media," but that doesn't necessarily mean partisanship. I'm against that, in fact. But my audience frankly wants more politics and, yes, more partisanship.

Air America has been criticized in some quarters for being a mouthpiece for the Democrats.

Air America began proudly in lockstep with the Democrats, it's true. But the real failure has been on the industry and advertising side, not necessarily the programming. Most professional ad agencies in the talk radio space had only worked with the right wing; after all, that's all there was. And left talk radio frightens corporations, because it is seen—rightly, perhaps—as being "outside the system." Corporations are afraid of anything unfamiliar or controversial. So I always felt the focus on Air America's content was misplaced—what was really broken there was in the back room and the executive offices.

Does advertisers' fear explain why conservatives dominate talk radio?

Only partially. The major reason is that right-wing talkers start on a network, on 300 stations or so. So they seem successful right from the start. Also you have to factor in the echo effect—many on the right have their own television shows extending their reach, along with newspaper columns, books, and so on. Plus someone like Hannity or Limbaugh, honestly, has a lot of skill in the radio medium.

Is there a place in radio for shock jocks like Don Imus?

To be the alter ego for things other people won't say out loud? Yes, of course. But you have to be smart about how you shock. Calling struggling young black women "ho's" is a whole other thing. People want to believe that none of this talk hurts, but in a society where nooses are still being hung, none of this is neutral. It's real-life people putting real-life obstacles in front of each other. Many people on the left are in denial and want to believe we are past this. But those girls on that basketball team didn't think so.

The liberal half of Fox News Channel's *Hannity & Colmes*, Alan Colmes is one of the most prominent liberal personalities on talk radio today. His radio show is syndicated on more than 70 terrestrial stations as well as satellite radio channels.

Can talk radio change people's minds?

Talk radio preaches to the choir. People tune in with a host they identify with. They may love the host or they may hate the host, but they like it. I think Bush has made more people change their minds than talk radio has.

Why do conservatives dominate the market?

A lot of it started with a paranoia on the part of conservatives that they were being excluded from the "mainstream" media. Another aspect is that conservatives tend to look at things in a very black-and-white way, versus liberals, who tend to bring more nuanced views. And that's an easier sell.

Will this change?

Air America has taken a stab at it. I've been on talk radio for a while and been successful at it. You can't lead by mission. I like to say that I'm a broadcaster who happens to be a liberal, not so much the other way around.

How will the Imus firing affect things?

It hasn't really affected me, because I didn't do the kinds of things that he did. It's been very bad for the industry. It's not a good sign when special interest groups, whether they be left or right, start making demands and the corporation buckles to what they demand.

Maddow hosts The Rachel Maddow Show weeknights on Air America. She is also a regular contributor to MSNBC's Countdown with Keith Olbermann.

How would you describe your style?
I was recently described in print as Amy Goodman with animal noises. I don't think that's exactly right, but there's an element of hard-core news.

How do you prepare for a program each day?
The rule of thumb in talk radio is that people prepare an hour for every hour that they're on the air. I do a two-hour show, and I get here every day at least six hours before my show starts. I read for most of that time.

When you begin your broadcast, do you adopt a different personality?
I can be in the worst mood in the entire world, or I can be tired, or jet-lagged, but I still feel like every minute I can be on the air is golden. It's literally exciting to me every day to have the chance to say what I think and explain the news.

How important is listener interaction to you?
I don't take calls regularly, the way that a lot of hosts do. I know that's controversial, but that's part of the decision to try to be real news-heavy, to be less discussion, more information.

Where do you see progressive radio going?
Air America has got the creative material to win. We're trying to do something that's wicked hard to do from a business perspective. But in terms of the talent and in terms of the shows that we're putting out there, I'd put us up against anybody. The bigwigs on the left—people who have money—ought to invest in us as a way of investing in liberal infrastructure. The enthusiasm is there, and so I'm pretty hopeful.

Former CNN news writer Mike Malloy broadcast for Air America from 2004 to 2006 and currently broadcasts for the Nova M Radio Network.

How do you describe your style on the radio?

I have no patience with Republicans or right-wingers and very little patience with people who are middle of the road. Jim Hightower said, "The only thing you find in the middle of the road is a yellow line and dead armadillos." The corruption and the utter incompetence of the Bush administration pisses me off to a degree I didn't know was possible. So I scream, I yell, I pound things, and occasionally I've been known to use bad language.

If a caller upsets you, do you just cut them off?

Over 20 years of talk radio, but especially in the past three or four years, I've found that most right-wing or conservative callers are functionally illiterate. Their minds are capable of parroting only what they've heard from Rush Limbaugh, or Free Republic, or Sean Hannity. They are incapable of carrying on a dialogue. I know that the majority of my audience doesn't want to hear this. They don't want to hear it, because they deal with it constantly out in the real world: at the workplace, in their churches, in their synagogues, on the bus, in the carpool, at the PTA meeting.

What do you like most about being on radio as compared to doing news writing?

Talk radio is all about injecting me, Mike Malloy, into the story: my personal, gut-level feelings about things. I also bring in what has funneled into me from the listeners via e-mail, letters, and phone calls. There's an awful lot of theater in the kind of talk radio that I do. And I think that's a good thing, to be able to translate the day's horrific political events into something that connects with people on an emotional level. If I can do that, then I feel like I'm doing what talk radio should be about.

People tend to use Rush Limbaugh as a yardstick when they talk about building a large audience for talk radio.

The genius of Rush Limbaugh was not Limbaugh; it was Roger Ailes. In the mid-'80s, Ailes, who went on to found Fox News Network, said to small and medium markets in places like Bowling Green and Albuquerque, "I have a three-hour program. It's on from noon to three, and it's conservative, so it'll gel well with your advertisers. And I'll give it to you free. All you have to do is give me X number of minutes per hour that I will, in turn, sell to national advertisers." Well, the small to medium markets salivated over that. It doesn't make any difference that Limbaugh is anti-American, he's anti-woman, he's anti-democratic process, he's anti-U.S. Constitution, he's pro-war, he's pro-death, he's pro–upper class. None of that matters. What matters is the program was free.

So we need to come up with a better marketing idea for progressive talk.

This society of ours is a marketing petri dish. The person who comes up with the best marketing idea wins, not the person who comes up with the best product. Right-wing talk radio is not a good product. It's toxic. It's destructive. It's negative. But it had behind it a marketing genius.

Former Air Force mechanic Rhodes has been syndicated by Air America since 2004.

Is it safe to say you represent the rage a lot of people feel about what's going on politically?
I'm not really angry; I'm frustrated beyond belief. And sometimes I'm just plain sickened. Katrina was sickening. The Iraq war—you look at it and you just can't believe it.

How does your military service inform your views?
I understand why people enlist. In my case my father said, "You're smart and you're not pretty. Men don't like that. You're not going to marry well. You need to get a job." So I drove over to Fort Hamilton and signed up for the Air Force.

So I understand why people join and why they're willing to surrender their civil rights. But I also understood the reason why the American military is the proudest and most fierce fighting force on the planet—because we feel like we're doing a legitimate job for a legitimate government. So it helps me understand the problems. It helps me understand the underfunding of the troops. They're not giving them the best equipment in the world. They're not giving them what they need to do their job.

You've expressed this sense of betrayal on the air.
I can't imagine being on foreign soil making $1,300 a month, with a family at home, car payments, and house payments, and the whole nine yards, and serving next to a private contractor who's getting 80 grand to pump gas. In my military experience, that can't happen.

You are gaining market share.
I'm number one in time spent listening in New York City, but I'm number 33 in how many people are listening. That's the company's job: to market the show, to bring the people in. My job is to entertain them once they're in the seats. I'm succeeding at my job.

What drives you crazy?

When people insist that they're right. The other day, I got something wrong and a woman called me up. In a very easy-to-follow, easy-to-research manner, she told me how I was getting it wrong. And I said to her, "I didn't know that. This is a good day. I learned something." I don't care if I'm wrong. I just care when people are wrong and insist that they're not.

You don't suffer fools.

No.

How do you gain the listeners' trust?

The power of radio is that it gets under your skin, it gets in your soul. The power of television is the visuals get in your head. People trust TV entirely too much. They think the news media is credible and that they'll never lie, they'll never distort. I don't get that. I don't know why people aren't more skeptical of the media they ingest, whether it's radio or TV. I'm always telling people, don't believe a word you hear, including me. Go look it up.

Miller is the host of the progressive *Stephanie Miller Show*, syndicated by Jones Radio Networks out of Los Angeles. She is the daughter of former U.S. Representative William E. Miller and a onetime actress and stand-up comedian.

How do you see your show?
Entertainment, period. It's not about right wing or left wing. The minute we think we're a political movement, we're dead. Every call or e-mail I get starts with, "I'm a right-winger, but I listen to you and I love you." Most people don't define themselves politically in everyday life.

How do you feel about the Fairness Doctrine?
I don't know that the Fairness Doctrine is the way to address the problem, but I think fairness is.

How is it that Hannity has so many markets?
Sean Hannity is really good. But the crappiest right-wing show can go out of the gate on 200 stations. There are a lot of Rush and Sean imitators out there, and many of them are just not as good. Do they deserve two, three hundred stations? No, in my opinion, probably not. But there are a lot of successful progressive talk shows around the country. The myth that every conservative radio show is successful and every progressive show is just not the truth. Everybody has spin.

What's the long-term Imus fallout?
I think it absolutely has contributed to a chilling environment. Radio is edgy and irreverent, that's the nature of talk radio. After Imus, it's gonna be a "gotcha" environment. You can record ten seconds of anybody's show and get them fired. What makes it worse is that a lot of people who hadn't even heard of Imus can go on YouTube and hear his comments. In the old days you used to call up and ask for the tapes, and the station would say, "No, I'm sorry, we didn't tape that."

CONCLUSION

Beyond Changing the Channel

You can't be neutral on a moving train. —Howard Zinn

People want to believe that none of this talk hurts, but in a society where nooses are still being hung, none of this is neutral.
—Laura Flanders

As this book went to press, talk radio's top shock jocks continued to make news on a daily basis. Rush Limbaugh and Laura Ingraham injected themselves into the presidential race (as well as the headlines) by launching "Operation Chaos," a campaign encouraging Republicans to "cross over" and vote for Hillary Clinton as a way to prolong her fight for the nomination and make it more difficult for Democrats to unite in the fall. Bill O'Reilly threatened to "join a lynch mob" against Michelle Obama, wife of Democratic candidate Barack Obama. And Don Imus prepared to host Republican presidential candidate John McCain on his resyndicated show, while his new employers, WABC-AM and Citadel Broadcasting, prepared to host the 19th annual Imus Radiothon benefit. Just one year after being unceremoniously yanked off the air by CBS Radio during the previous Radiothon, the I-Man was definitively back in his full, syndicated, simulcast, save-the-children glory.

Meanwhile, in an eerie echo of the Imus controversy, racist remarks by Michael Savage on *The Savage Nation* led to a successful public campaign that convinced sponsors to pull their advertising from the widely syndicated show. In response, according to an account in the *New York Times*, Savage began broadcasting from three "virtual safehouses" in undisclosed locations and warned that he "is licensed to carry a pistol and does so."

Among the reasons Savage reportedly "feared for his life" were his continual verbal assaults on wide swaths of minorities. While discussing President Bush's plan to increase spending to combat AIDS in Africa by $30 billion, Savage responded to a caller's criticisms with a series of derogatory remarks about the caller, Africa, and Africans. The caller, identified only as Kojo, asked Savage if he knew how AIDS got to Africa.

"It got there because it was spread from eating green monkey meat, my friend. If you study the science—but I don't think you have the capacity to understand science, my dear friend, Kojo," responded the mean-spirited shock jock.

Savage continued in starkly racist terms: "There's immigration for you. There's the new America for you. Bring them in by the millions. Bring in 10 million more from Africa. Bring them in with AIDS. Show how multicultural you are. They can't reason, but bring them in with a machete in their head. Go ahead. Bring them in with machetes in their mind."

Talk radio continued to make big financial news as well, as Clear Channel Communications, the nation's largest radio station owner, moved closer to the completion of its $19.5 billion sale to private investors. The Texas-based company grew into a media giant following passage of the 1996 telecommunications law that ended the national limit on how many radio stations a single company may own. Thankfully, those times may now be a-changing.

When Clear Channel Communications applied for FCC approval of the sale, the company held licenses to 1,172 radio stations and 35 television stations nationwide. In order for the new owners to comply with redefined FCC limits, the company agreed to sell more than 40 radio stations in top markets. (Clear Channel was originally exempted or "grandfathered" from the law, but the exemption did not apply to the new owners.) FCC officials said transfer of control of the stations was "in the public interest" and would "improve competition." Even after selling an additional 448 stations in smaller markets, and spinning off its TV stations in a separate deal, the new owners will still control more than 500 individual local radio stations.

The ascendancy of John McCain as the Republicans' choice for president caused yet another twist in the topsy-turvy right-wing talk radio world. Although by most measures one of the most conservative members of Congress, McCain has long been vilified by the even more conservative talkmeisters for taking positions that differ from theirs on issues such as taxes, immigration, and campaign finance reform. Thus when he began to emerge as the GOP presidential front-runner, McCain became the target of a fresh round of attacks—most notably from Grand Poobah Rush Limbaugh.

Thrusting himself back into the news cycle by delivering what he cheekily called his "nonconcession speech," Limbaugh assailed McCain's candidacy. "There was no figure in our roster of candidates who rose up to challenge him or galvanize conservative support," Limbaugh said. "All the candidates on our side, for various reasons, are uninspiring or worse—and so, just as I predicted, the base has fractured."

Limbaugh complained vociferously that McCain was "not the choice of conservatives, as opposed to the choice of the Republican establishment—and that distinction is key. The Republican establishment, which has long sought to rid the party of conservative influence since Reagan, is feeling a victory today, as well as our friends in the media. But both are just far-fetched and wrong." Acolytes such as Sean Hannity, Laura Ingraham, and Mark Levin joined in denouncing McCain.

After John McCain had secured the Republican nomination, Limbaugh and his ilk turned their attention once again to the Democrats. But when the *New York Times* published an investigative article that was widely construed as an attempt to damage McCain, right-wing talkers eased up on their attacks. In turn, McCain began to grant them increased access and to reappear on their airwaves.

Time will tell if Limbaugh or any of the other conservative talkers will continue to target John McCain. But by blaming first the "Republican establishment" (Senator McCain) and then "the media" (the *New York Times*) for betraying "true" conservatism, Limbaugh enjoyed a two-pronged success: he promoted himself and his program, and he reenergized his own base—his listeners.

Right-wing talk radio is as much a movement as a media phenomenon—one fueled by deep-seated perceptions of victimization and voicelessness. Conservative talkers' condemnation of the very conservative McCain—as well as their appeals to listeners to vote for Hillary Clinton—may seem bizarre to outsiders, and particularly to progressives. But in the historical context of right-wing talk radio, it makes perfect sense. McCain refused to toe their predetermined party line, and therefore he had to be punished—as were Trent Lott and others before him.

Limbaugh's treatment of McCain is best understood as a potent combination of performance, politics, and punishment. This course of action is carefully choreographed, with the goal of keeping Rush Limbaugh front and center in a reinvigoration of conservative talk—no matter *who* ends up in the White House. Years of enjoying top access to the corridors of power have brought benefits and blandishments, but inevitably co-opted the movement, making it soft and compliant. Limbaugh now proposes, prophetlike, to lead the faithful back to the rigors of the wilderness where right-wing talk radio was born and eventually thrived. So conservative talkers are readying themselves and their audiences to assume the familiar mantle of victimhood and howl once again with the rage of embittered outsiders.

Clearly, talk radio's top shock jocks know how to generate publicity for themselves and their programs, stir up listeners, and put pressure on politicians—all of which is their right under the First Amendment. Too often, however, their impact extends far beyond their own admittedly niche audience share and out into the generalized media marketplace. Mainstream corporate media outlets frequently amplify and even adopt the shock jocks' reactionary messages, "reporting" (and repeating) each fresh comment and outrage, while simultaneously weaving it into an overall narrative meant for mass consumption. This "apolitical" commercial news processing inevitably increases the conservatives' ability to spread their opinions, false information, and misleading memes and themes (such as "Barack *Hussein* Obama is secretly a Muslim!") throughout the larger media system.

Having grown in both influence and audience, progressive talk radio has begun to push back against the worst excesses of radical right-wing talk. The left talkers are also finding themselves accompanied for the first time by a nascent and newly potent independent media infrastructure. With the Internet as a sort of progressive counterpart to conservative talk radio, there are now literally hundreds of aggressive left-leaning blogs, many written by top journalists, as well as progressive news-aggregating Web sites such as Huffington Post, AlterNet (publisher of this book), Salon, Raw Story, Buzzflash, Common Dreams, and others. These sites draw millions of visitors each month.

This independent media challenge not only confronts dangerous hate speech but also tackles the echoes and distortions that lead to an information gap for consumers of both corporate and conservative media in the United States. Research shows that increased independent media consumption—from NPR to news-oriented blogs and Web sites to progressive magazines—keeps citizens better informed. A case in point: a 2003 study conducted by the Program on International Policy Attitudes at the University of Maryland concluded that Americans' opinions are shaped in large part by which news outlet they rely on. Researchers explained, "The extent of Americans' misperceptions vary significantly, depending on their source of news. Those who receive most of their news from Fox News are more likely than average to have misperceptions. Those who receive most of their news from NPR or PBS are less likely to have misperceptions."

The Citizen Response to Hate Radio

This book is primarily concerned with communicating the evils of shock jock radio, which have been presented in much of their gory detail. But it is equally important that listeners and media consumers come to understand that such hate talk can be confronted and successfully challenged. If you're concerned about the astonishing amount of hate speech being spewed on the public airwaves, the near-monopoly of conservative-leaning viewpoints, the deliberate blurring of borders between news, information, opinion, and entertainment, it's not enough, as some suggest, simply to change the channel. There are many models and campaigns that have already taken on the monsters of hate talk and won important victories.

Hate speech over public airwaves isn't just "politically incorrect." Left unopposed, it leads to real acts of hate visited on real people. (Those who doubt this phenomenon might study the use of radio in the genocidal psychosis of Rwanda, or Slobodan Milosevic's cunning use of the media to whip up murderous nationalist anger and actions in the Balkans.) An imbalance of political viewpoints in the media fosters feelings of exclusion on all sides and ever-growing partisanship that distorts our political process to its detriment. Our democratic society ultimately depends on an informed citizenry, yet our citizens are increasingly *uninformed* living in a media environment where even the most basic facts are spun, together with opinion, conjecture, and demagoguery, into thin gossamer baskets of political talking points. As a society, we can't afford to simply stand by. We need to take action.

What We Can Do: Five Ways to Challenge Hate Talk Media and Strengthen the Alternatives

1. Support Independent Media

We all know how much and how often the mass media fails us. We also know that a wide range of progressive media is accurate and dependable. We need to support independent journalists and journalism rather than continue to accept factually challenged opinions and hate-filled entertainment. You can start by consuming more independent media. Pass it on to your friends, and urge them to be both creative contributors and financial supporters of independent media.

In addition to progressive public and community radio, there is a vast array of other forms of media—much of it on the Internet—to keep us stimulated and informed. A handful of my favorites in the world of independent media are briefly profiled here, but literally hundreds of other worthy and easily accessible media entities are available. Make your own list of what you watch, read, and listen to, and share it with friends. Bookmark reliably informative Web sites, and use RSS feeds to create your own personal indie media empire to help you keep up with the news from a wide range of diverse perspectives.

2. Demand Media Accountability

Progressives have a long tradition of monitoring and holding media accountable for what they say and how they cover the news. There are many tactics for successful media monitoring, including letter writing, protests, and boycotts. There are also a number of groups that effectively pressure corporate media to do a better job. Among the best is Fairness and Accuracy in Reporting. FAIR, which has been around for decades, produces the popular magazine *Extra!,* the *Counterspin* radio program, and a helpful Web site, and has spawned a number of progressive leaders and media personalities, including Laura Flanders and Jeff Cohen.

More recently, former right-winger David Brock (author of *Blinded by the Right: The Conscience of an Ex-Conservative*) helped create Media Matters for America, which quickly became an important source of primary information for media watchers of all sorts by dint of documenting and disseminating much of the hate talk that pervades the media. Free Press, the largest media reform organization in the United States, is another good resource. By promoting diverse and independent media ownership, strong public media, and universal access to communications, and by engaging citizens in policy debates and demands for better media, it has proved invaluable since its inception in 2002. Finally, I urge you to visit MediaChannel.org, which I helped found in 2000.

Remember—watchdogs do more than just watch. Become active in the national media reform movement. Demand regulatory and structural changes that will lead to more localism, more choices, and more voices within the radio industry. Contact the FCC and let the commissioners know about your concerns. Attend the many FCC hearings on issues of importance to you. And don't forget to file complaints with the FCC every time you hear hate speech on talk radio. Remember, use of our airwaves is only licensed to corporations, and those licenses are periodically reviewed and renewed—or not, depending on the licensee's behavior.

3. Go After the Profiteers of Hate

Let the owners of the major media companies know that you oppose their hate-laced content. Make it clear to advertisers and sponsors that you won't buy their products if they continue to support antidemocratic and un-American hate speech. If your initial responses are met with scorn or (more likely) simply ignored, work in concert with others to ratchet up the pressure. Organize public protests such as letter-writing campaigns, online petitions, real-world picket lines, or whatever you find most effective in the battle against the shock jocks and their corporate backers. A number of successful campaigns have been launched against advertisers on hate shows, most notably the sponsors of Don Imus and Michael Savage.

Sometimes it can make sense to enlist employees of the offending media firms in your cause. They're not your enemies, and in fact they may be as appalled by what their companies are doing as you are. Employee protest at NBC was a key factor is swaying executives at the General Electric–owned news operation to remove Don Imus from his MSNBC cable television program. Another tactic that has had some success is buying small amounts of stock in the companies, attending annual meetings, and organizing sympathetic fellow shareholders to speak out against hate speech. Finally, attacking the bottom line of the companies that make millions in profits with hate talk media may be effective, especially if organized on a large scale. Consider boycotts of goods and services sold by the offending corporations. In talk radio, as in most businesses, money talks—and when moral suasion, public shaming, and opprobrium prove ineffective, a threat to the bottom line can work wonders.

4. Fight Hate Anywhere You Find It

Commit to speaking out against hate speech wherever you encounter it, whether in the mass media or in your daily life. Silence can be construed as acceptance, or even complicity, so if you hear hate speech, let the speakers know they are not speaking in your name.

There are also many important national groups that invest time and resources in fighting hate, frequently using the media for their organizing efforts. Here are three of my favorites:

The National Council of La Raza (NCLR), the largest national Hispanic civil rights and advocacy group in the country, launched the Wave of Hope campaign in January 2008 to take the hate out of the national debate on immigration. This robust effort includes the Web site WeCanStopTheHate.org, which educates around hate speech and its consequences. The campaign also engages media networks and political candidates to separate themselves from hate groups and hate speech. NCLR argues that media celebrities and the growth of talk radio have contributed significantly to the unprecedented use of hate speech on the airwaves. The group maintains that unchecked hate speech has a dangerous effect on the daily lives of communities of color, on immigration policy, and on the fairness of the current immigration debate.

The Southern Poverty Law Center (SPLC) is a civil rights law firm founded in 1971 that combats discrimination and hate. Over the course of its history, SPLC has won significant legal battles, tracked the movements and activities of hate groups, and launched an innovative educational program teaching tolerance to children. SPLC has also worked to halt paramilitary training by hate groups, protect migrant workers, and in general curb the activities of extremists.

Not in Our Town (NIOT) is a nationwide project (for which I volunteer) that promotes tolerance through grassroots community dialogue, organizing, and action. The project was inspired by a 1994 documentary that chronicled the inspirational response of residents of Billings, Montana, to a spate of hate crimes in their community. Following a series of crimes targeting Jewish and Native American residents, the community organized large-scale rallies, marches, and vigils to protest discrimination, intolerance, and hate. NIOT has since promoted this model of grassroots organizing in communities throughout the country. Get involved by hosting public screenings of documentaries, petitioning public figures to draft and sign proclamations decrying hate, bringing educational materials into the classroom, and holding conference workshops. For more information, visit pbs.org/niot/get_involved/index.html.

5. Find and Share Quality Journalism

Just as it's true that the best cure for hate speech is more speech, the best antidote to poor journalism is quality journalism. There's a way to find and share quality journalism online by becoming a member of a social news network such as NewsTrust.net (of which I am editorial director). This Web site features free daily feeds of news and opinion that are carefully reviewed by community members. NewsTrust reviewers rate the news based on quality, not just popularity, using core journalistic principles such as fairness, evidence, sourcing, and context. The nonprofit, nonpartisan project also provides news literacy tools and a trust network to help citizens make informed decisions about democracy.

There are a number of ways to influence and change the American media system, including confronting the mass media about their many transgressions, protecting the Internet from corporate control, and adopting one or more various legislative or regulatory strategies for media reform. But monitoring the media and working for reform are only part of the answer. Some observers even believe it can lead progressives to view themselves as powerless victims of "overbearing corporate media ownership concentration." If we accept the message that little can change until the corporate media is "reformed" and the system is somehow "democratized," little *will* change, at least in the foreseeable future. We should also focus on competing in the marketplaces of commerce and ideas, and transforming the way the funders and investors think about media. As Peter Leyden of the New Politics Institute has noted, the "progressive political community needs to recognize the integral linkage between changes in media and changes in politics."

In the end, the most powerful form of media reform will be to strengthen the independent media enough so it can compete head-to-head with the hatemongering right-wing broadcast media. To reach parity and bring full competition to the media marketplace, progressives will need a large-scale increase in media capacity building. To accomplish that, progressive funders and investors must be convinced to abandon previous assumptions and to increase their support of the kind of media that is a direct antidote to the radical right—as expressed most vociferously on conservative talk radio airwaves.

Like politics, all media is local. So along with demonstrating, boycotting, and speaking out, consider exposing yourself to some new viewpoints to supplement and challenge your own. If you lean to the left, check out some of the less-strident conservative talk show hosts, such as Mike Gallagher, or even libertarians like John Ziegler and Michael Reagan. If you're a conservative or an independent, expose yourself to progressive media networks like Air America. Who knows? You may learn something you didn't know.

If you haven't already, become more civically engaged and politically involved, and let your fellow citizens, as well as candidates for office, know of your concern about media-related issues, including deregulation and consolidation, phony news and paid opinions, and hate speech masquerading as humor anywhere on the public airwaves.

In sum, use your free speech to encourage more free speech on your airwaves. In the final analysis, that's the only way to create and sustain a media system that will function in the service of democracy and the people. You'll find that by helping heal America, you'll be helping yourself. After all, the airwaves and the country you save will be your own.

AN INDIE MEDIA FEAST

In addition to sampling the rapidly growing progressive radio world, your daily media diet can include a cornucopia of other terrific independent media sources—blogs, Web sites, print magazines, television and video outlets, and activist campaigns. Here's a taste of just a few.

INTERNET NEWS AND OPINION
Huffingtonpost.com, AlterNet.org, Commondreams.org, Salon.com

INDEPENDENT TELEVISION
Link TV, Free Speech TV (with Laura Flanders), The Real News

BLOGS
Talking Points Memo, **TalkingPointsMemo.com**
Open Left, **OpenLeft.com**
Think Progress, **ThinkProgress.org**
Carpetbagger Report, **TheCarpetBaggerReport.com**
All Spin Zone, **AllSpinZone.com**
Feministe, **Feministe.blogspot.com**
Cliff Schecter, **Agonist.org/schechter/**
Pensito Review, **PensitoReview.com**
Fire Dog Lake, **FireDogLake.com**
Pam's House Blend, **PamsHouseBlend.com**

MAGAZINES
Mother Jones, Adbusters, the *Nation;* the *Progressive; In These Times*

ACTIVIST MEDIA CAMPAIGNS
Brave New Films. Brave New Films uses hard-hitting Internet video campaigns to challenge corporate media and encourage political action. Its work revamps the grassroots organizing model, making it possible for people to be informed and take action faster. Brave New Films's "No Savage" campaign encourages people to put pressure on businesses that advertise on *The Savage Nation*. "Choosing to support or not to support a business due to what they stand for or where they advertise, reflects the very highest ideals of American democracy and freedom of expression," says the "No Savage" campaign Web site.

Truth to Power Media. In his book *Savage Lies: The Half-Truths, Distortions and Outright Lies of a Right-Wing Blowhard*, journalist Bill Bowman provided a much-needed analysis of Savage's tactics of misinformation. Bowman's blog, TruthToPowerMedia.com, continues to expose Savage's sloppy research, outright lies, and distortions of facts. Truth to Power Media shreds Savage on a daily basis, showing that just a single dedicated media activist can do a lot to tarnish the reputation of a major shock jock.

Council on American-Islamic Relations. CAIR's mission is to enhance the understanding of Islam, protect civil liberties, and build coalitions that promote justice and mutual understanding. After Michael Savage called the Qur'an a "hateful little book" and said, "I don't want to hear one more word about Islam. Take your religion and shove it," CAIR led a boycott asking people not to patronize businesses that advertise on *The Savage Nation*. The boycott succeeded in convincing several companies to withdraw their advertising.

Hate Hurts America. The Hate Hurts America Interfaith and Community Coalition is an alliance of religious and civic organizations that came together to tackle the rise of anti-immigrant, antiminority rhetoric. Functioning primarily through its Web site, HateHurtsAmerica.org, the coalition argues that, while hatemongers have a First Amendment right to spew their hate speech, Americans of all backgrounds have a First Amendment right not to support it. "We therefore call upon companies to withdraw their advertisements from *The Savage Nation* as a concrete demonstration of support for the American traditions of religious and cultural tolerance and mutual respect," says the Hate Hurts America Web site.

ACKNOWLEDGMENTS

I am grateful to a great number of individuals for their assistance in the preparation and production of this book. First on the list is my able assistant and researcher Aaron Cutler, who did yeoman-like work throughout the months that we labored together.

I am also thankful to Don Hazen, executive director of the Independent Media Institute, first for asking me to be a columnist on AlterNet.org and then for conceiving of this book and encouraging me to write it; to Rachel Neumann, Tai Moses, and Elijah Nella for their editorial and production work; and to my colleagues at Globalvision, Inc., and MediaChannel.org, especially my partner Danny Schechter, webmaster David DeGraw, and our talented and efficient "Chief of Stuff" Pat Horstman, as well as to the many other employees, associates, trainees, and volunteers who have assisted in our work there.

In the course of researching and writing this book, we reached out to a large number of participants in and observers of the talk radio industry. Chief among them, of course, were the top radio talk show hosts. Sadly, but not surprisingly, most simply assumed the work would be a "liberal hit job," as one potential interviewee phrased it, and none of those mentioned in this book—from Rush Limbaugh and Sean Hannity to Bill O'Reilly and Michael Savage, et al.—was willing to talk.

Nevertheless, a number of other radio talk show hosts—some quite conservative in their politics, some not—fearlessly agreed to be interviewed, and I am grateful to all of them, including Michael Reagan, Mike Gallagher, Michael Smerconish, John Ziegler, John Gambling, Stephanie Miller, Alan Colmes, and Cenk Uygur. In addition, I am most thankful to Mark Karlin and his associates at Buzzflash.com for allowing us to reprint portions of interviews with Randi Rhodes, Mike Malloy, Thom Hartmann, and Rachel Maddow, which first appeared in their entirety on Buzzflash.

I also wish to thank others who agreed to be interviewed, including John Moyers, whose TomPaine.com Web site published important early work by Philip Nobile outlining a long history of ill-considered remarks by talk show host Don Imus; veteran talk show producer Jill Vitale, who worked for years with Sean Hannity and now with John Gambling; and Ben Greenman, *New Yorker* editor and talk show listener par excellence. I am also indebted to Michael Harrison, editor and publisher of the leading trade publication *Talkers Magazine*, for his interview and many insights, as well as for permission to reprint *Talkers'* 2008 "Top Talk Radio Audiences" and "Heavy Hundred" compilations. Thanks also to Bruce McCall for permission to reprint his very funny *New Yorker* humor piece on liberal talk radio; to J. Max Robins, formerly of *Broadcasting & Cable* magazine; to Dennis Wharton and Eva Henninger of the National Association of Broadcasters; and to Renee Cassis of the Radio Advertising Bureau. I am particularly indebted as well to Alison Humes for her excellent editorial notes and overall emotional support.

I would also like to acknowledge gratefully the work of many others who labor in the necessary field of media reform and monitoring, including those at Fairness and Accuracy in Reporting, Media Matters for America, Free Press, and the Center for American Progress, whose study *The Structural Imbalance of Political Talk Radio* is cited extensively here. And I wish to thank my many friends and colleagues in the media and democracy movement worldwide, who continue to push for free speech, not hate speech on the public airwaves, along with more voices, more choices, greater diversity, and more democracy in all the global media.

Finally, to my sons Ciaran and Aidan, as they face an unfolding future of as-yet-undreamed-of communications possibilities, always remember: "Media is a plural."

—Rory O'Connor,
April 2008

RORY O'CONNOR

Documentary filmmaker and journalist Rory O'Connor is cofounder and president of the international media firm Globalvision, Inc., and board chair of The Global Center, an affiliated nonprofit foundation. He is also editorial director of the social news network NewsTrust.net. A regular columnist for AlterNet.org and MediaChannel, O'Connor also writes the popular "Media Is a Plural" blog, accessible at Roryoconnor.org. His broadcast, film, and print work has been honored with a George Polk Award, a Writers Guild Award, a George Orwell Award, and two Emmys, among other awards.

AARON CUTLER

Bryn Mawr, Pennsylvania, native Aaron Cutler attended Friends' Central School for 13 years before enrolling at Brown University. He is currently a senior double-majoring in English and literary arts, Brown's name for creative writing. Regardless of where he is or what he does next year, he will be sure to listen to conservative talk radio.

AlterNet.org is an award-winning news magazine and online community that creates original journalism and amplifies the best of dozens of other independent media sources. Its mission is to inspire citizen action and advocacy on the environment, human rights and civil liberties, social justice, media, and health care issues. AlterNet's editorial mix underscores a commitment to fairness, equity, and global stewardship, and to making connections across generational, ethnic, and issue lines. Its aim is to stimulate, motivate, and engage. AlterNet has won two Webby Awards for "Best Web Magazine" and several Independent Press Awards for online political coverage. AlterNet was also named one of National Public Radio's five "Winners on the Internet."

AlterNet Books was created to bring our readers a deeper and more insightful analysis of the progressive issues that matter. Launched with *Young Dick Cheney: Great American,* AlterNet Books is a source of provocative thinking and high-quality writing. *Shock Jocks: Hate Speech and Talk Radio* is our second book. In the fall, we will be churning out three more books. Coming out just in time for the November elections, *Count My Vote: Getting Your Vote Right for 2008* will outline new voting technology developments and prepare the voting public to navigate a process that has proved disastrous in the past. *Water Consciousness: Everything You Need to Know to Protect the World's Most Precious Resource* is a comprehensive, solution-focused guide to the world's greatest environmental crisis. *The Illegal Job Scam: The Real Truth Behind Immigration Wars* offers a radically different vision of how progressives can approach the stalled immigration debate in America. Visit https://alternet.org/books today!

green press
INITIATIVE

Independent Media Institute is committed to preserving ancient forests and natural resources. We elected to print this title on 30% post consumer recycled paper, processed chlorine free. As a result, for this printing, we have saved:

14 Trees (40' tall and 6-8" diameter)
4,938 Gallons of Wastewater
9 million BTU's of Total Energy
634 Pounds of Solid Waste
1,190 Pounds of Greenhouse Gases

Independent Media Institute made this paper choice because our printer, Thomson-Shore, Inc., is a member of Green Press Initiative, a nonprofit program dedicated to supporting authors, publishers, and suppliers in their efforts to reduce their use of fiber obtained from endangered forests.

For more information, visit www.greenpressinitiative.org

Environmental impact estimates were made using the Environmental Defense Paper Calculator. For more information visit: www.papercalculator.org.